Reclaiming Your Story

Reclaiming Your Story

*Family History
and
Spiritual Growth*

Merle R. Jordan

Westminster John Knox Press
Louisville, Kentucky

Scripture quotations from the New Revised Standard Version of the Bible are copyright © 1989 by the Division of Christian Education of the National Council of the Churches of Christ in the U.S.A. and are used by permission.

Scripture quotations from the Amplified Bible are used by permission. Old Testament copyright © 1965, 1987 by The Zondervan Corporation. The Amplified New Testament copyright 1958, 1987 by The Lockman Foundation.

Excerpts from *Object Relations in Severe Trauma: Psychotherapy of the Sexually Abused Child* by Stephen Prior, Ph.D., Psy.D., copyright © 1996 by Stephen Prior, have been reprinted with permission of the publisher, Jason Aronson Inc.

Excerpts from "Prayer and Meditation in Pastoral Care and Counseling" by Merle Jordan, in *Handbook for Basic Types of Care and Counseling,* ed. Howard Stone and William Clements, copyright © 1991 Abingdon Press, have been reprinted with permission of the publisher.

Excerpts from *Your Sacred Self* by Wayne W. Dyer, copyright © 1995 by Wayne W. Dyer, have been reprinted by permission of HarperCollins Publishers, Inc.

Book design by Sharon Adams
Cover design by Pam Poll
Cover art 1998 PhotoDisc, Inc.

First Edition
Published by Westminster John Knox Press
Louisville, Kentucky

This book is printed on acid-free paper that meets the American National Standards Institute Z39.48 standard. ∞

PRINTED IN THE UNITED STATES OF AMERICA

99 00 01 02 03 04 05 06 07 08 — 10 9 8 7 8 6 5 4 3 2

Cataloging-in-Publication data for this book may be obtained from the Library of Congress.

ISBN 0-664-25641-4

*Lovingly dedicated to my family of origin,
who provided the context for my life and growth,
and to my beloved wife Barbara, whose insight
and love help me transform my spiritual life*

Contents

INTRODUCTION

᭝᭝᭝᭝᭝᭝᭝᭝᭝

Spirituality is the journey out of the microcosm into the macrocosm. —*Henri Nouwen*

Your family of origin is the microcosm in which your relationships with self, others, and God are initially formed. Thus it is imperative to take seriously the context of your family of origin as the crucible in which your emotional and spiritual experience takes shape. Your patterns of interpersonal communication, intimacy, defenses, and behavior are largely learned in your family of origin, and those dynamics tend to strongly influence your relationship with God. In addition to basing your initial mental representations of God on the perceived nature and quality of human relationships in your family, your own concept of self and the roles you play in life are largely determined by the feelings, values, and beliefs of authority figures that you internalize from your childhood family.

A central argument of this book is that deep spiritual transformation may better occur when you have differentiated from your family of origin so that you harbor no ultimate loyalties that would block a total commitment to God in Christ. The heart of this thesis comes from Jesus' words: "Whoever comes to me and does not hate father and mother, wife and children, brothers and sisters, yes, and even life itself, cannot be my disciple."[1] This statement is Jesus' emphatic way of stating that true differentiation from close human authority figures and relationships is essential for discipleship. There is to be no other god before God.

The corollary to this statement is that you may become fixated upon some images of childhood authority which you impute with ultimate authority. Therefore, you must detach yourself from these internalized images or psychic idols so that your deepest affection and attachment can find their object in God.

Carl Jung wrote, "The more intensively the family has stamped its character upon the child, the more (the child) will tend to feel and see its earlier miniature world again in the bigger world of adult life."[2] Doing family of origin work is a way of being in charge of the leftovers from the past so that you can be "better able to create for yourself the kind of life you want."[3] In this work, the goal is to change yourself and not others. The purpose is to liberate yourself from ultimate attachment to earthly authorities and affections so that you can be free to orient your center of being around an eternal Loving Being.

My late friend and colleague Calvin Turley used to say that pathology either was the result of or a case of mistaken identity. What he meant was that we sometimes derive our definition of self from dysfunctional authorities such as parents and incorporate that false appraisal of ourselves into our operative beliefs about who we really are. The false self, as defined by these negative authorities, functions as if it is the true self and the authentic identity of an individual. Some children perceive their identity as the bad child, the rejected child, the unwanted child, or the evil child of truth-telling parents, when what they are incorporating are actually distortions, lies, unjust criticism, blaming, and shaming. As we will see later, a method called narrative therapy can shed light on the psychological deceptions caused by the false authorities that you accept as the source of your genuine story, script, or truth about yourself, your identity, and your place in the world. The idea is that you need to reauthor the story of your life from God's perspective so that your worth and identity are determined by the true ultimate Authority, and not by false absolutes. All too few people can enjoy and live out the truth of Anthony de Mello's well-known phrase, "Behold God beholding you . . . and smiling."[4] Your attempt to incorporate the divine perspective of the self is a significant part of the transformation process of how you view yourself and live out your life. Philosopher J. V. Langmead Casserley said, "The more profound our sense of the reality and the meaning of Divinity, the more vivid our apprehension of the unique status and dignity of human personality."[5]

"Authoring" and "reauthoring" have the same root meaning as the word "authority." Therefore, in reauthoring your spiritual life, you need to be able to confront the false authorities that have ill-defined your value and identity, which the true Authority defines with love, respect, and care.

While standing on the ocean shore recently, I saw a young man and an older man row a small boat out to a larger one that was anchored offshore. The older man went to the wheel of the large boat and started the engine. Pulling in the anchor was not easy even for the younger sailor. But it was clear that the older man could not move the boat forward on its intended course until his sailing partner had hauled aboard the anchor. What a perfect metaphor for this book! We are all anchored in the personal histories we inherit from a family of origin, even when an adoptive or foster family may have played that role for us. Many of the meanings of our attachments to the significant childhood authorities who have helped to shape our lives are anchored in the ocean depths of our unconscious. Human attachments that have been internalized in the depths of our minds (often called "internalized objects") are significant in the development of our spiritual life or in its arrested development. Our maps of reality; images of God; values, beliefs, and meaning systems; patterns of relating, communicating, and interacting; sense of identity and self-worth; and emotional awareness and means of expression are largely determined by our relationships and experiences in our families of origin. We often need help from others to pull up our anchors from the past so that we can move forward on the journey that is truly ours.

In the pages that follow, I will begin by offering my spiritual autobiography. Since I am inviting you to reflect on your childhood history and its influence on your spiritual life, it is important that I name how I came to this place myself. In subsequent chapters I will outline methods for understanding how the roles and patterns from your family of origin may have influenced your relationship with the Divine. I will appraise some new and challenging ideas from secular sources that may help us understand the tenacious hold our childhood histories have over us, and some resources that can help us transform these patterns. I will address the problems that occur when we bring our family dynamics into our work life, our church leadership roles, and our caregiving relationships. And finally, I will try to help you understand a double idolatry that you may be caught in as an expression of your history, and on learning how to overcome this idolatry.

I acknowledge the tremendous help and support that I have received from various people in my spiritual pilgrimage, including therapists and spiritual directors. Since much of the reauthoring of my spirituality has taken place in the fifth and sixth decades of my life, I hope that will be encouraging to others who are at that point in their lives.

WHOSE ARE YOU?

▲▲▲▲▲▲▲▲

*H*ow do you, Lord, look at me? What do you
feel in your heart for me?   —John Eagan, S.J.

Introduction

Disclosing the patterns from my own family of origin is the best
way I know to help others begin exploring their family history.
I encourage you to adopt a questioning and curious mindset
so that you may discover how the experiences in the intimate
human relationships of your childhood establish subtle patterns of behavior and belief that shape the ways you relate to
God.

An Autobiographical Spiritual Journey

Let me first set the stage with the characters who are involved
in this implicitly theological drama. When I was born, my
mother contracted scarlet fever in the hospital, where she and I
remained for five and a half weeks, until she died. While I have
no conscious memory of her, I have become aware that I have a
kind of "tissue memory" (a memory in my body and being beyond one's usual rational memory) of that struggle in those
early weeks of my life. My father, who loved her dearly, was a
good and hard-working man who never spoke one word to me
about my mother; he died when I was twenty years old. I believe

that somewhere deep in his heart, he struggled with profound guilt because, while his mother-in-law had wanted her daughter to have the baby at home, he had insisted that I be born in the hospital, where my mother got sick and died. I think too that he was highly ambivalent about me because somehow he identified me as the cause of his wife's death. My sister was two years older than I was, and she naturally had a bond with both our birth mother and our father. She was very special to my father, and some people in the family, including my sister herself, felt that she had him wrapped around her little finger. My stepmother came into the picture shortly after I was brought home from the hospital. She was a practical nurse who lived next door, and she came into the house to take care of my sister and me. A few months later, to the apparent dismay of some of my father's family, she married my father. However, I once overheard her saying, "I don't know if I married the man or the baby." What she probably meant was that, although it was a relatively peaceful marriage, it was not a close and fulfilling emotional relationship for her. She found great satisfaction in being a mother and taking care of the children. Unfortunately, there was significant conflict between her and my sister, so I became closer to the center of her emotional world. In addition, I was close to my stepmother's sister, who was my favorite relative. My stepmother's parents were my only close grandparents; my grandfather, in particular, was unconditionally loving.

The context for my family of origin was a small city in Maine, where my father, who was really a farmer at heart, worked with one of his brothers in a service station. Perhaps he lost both loves in his life: his beloved first wife and farming. My stepmother gave up her career in practical nursing to be a homemaker and mother. She was close to her parents and to her sister, who lived together. I was often with them for Saturday evening dinners, holidays, and for weekends at my aunt's camp during the summer.

My frightened worldview and erroneous map of reality, including my distorted images of God, were the consequences of three major traumas. The first of these formative factors was the death of my birth mother. While I was not conscious of its impact until midlife, it laid the groundwork for deep separation anxiety, terrors of abandonment, and fear of rejection, judgment, and criticism, along with the fear that such abandonment was truly ultimate reality and would be the eternal reality for me. The second factor, which I also was largely unconscious of until my middle years, was that my father implicitly blamed me for the death of my mother. In some sense, I internalized an image of myself as a "murderer" who had to atone by being extra-responsible and good. The implicit blame and the fear of my father's criticism left me vulnerable to the power of other people. I tended to give power away to other people and to be a people pleaser because I could not bear feelings of rejection and judgment. The third factor was the emotional hypersensitivity of my stepmother, who loved me dearly and probably rescued me from a "failure to thrive" as an infant. However, her own needs for affirmation, love, and appreciation for her excellent mothering of me involved some controlling and manipulation. Total loyalty and enmeshment meant giving up my freedom to be independent within the relationship. Thus, I learned early to be a "parentified child."

When I was about six, my stepmother told me, with tears rolling down her cheeks, that although she believed that she was my mother and she loved me very much, I needed to know that my birth mother had died when I was an infant. She was visibly shaken when she said, "I'm afraid that you won't love me anymore as your mother, while I feel like I am your mother." I was shocked and bewildered, but I clearly got the message that I needed to take care of my stepmother, and so, from that day forward, I never asked her or my father a question about my birth mother. I lived in a conspiracy of silence about significant issues. The secrets were monstrous.

Conspiracy of Silence

The many dimensions of my family's conspiracy of silence had a serious impact on the feelings and needs I could be aware of in myself, share with others, or bring in prayer to God. Loyalty to my stepmother required that I have no questions and no feelings about my birth mother. It was clear that I would injure my stepmother if I showed any interest in my birth mother. I was not to grieve, be upset, or ask what my birth mother was like. Likewise, it was clear that my father did not want to address anything in regard to my birth mother. He and I never spoke one word about her, not even when he was on his deathbed. I had only a slight connection with my Nana, my birth mother's mother, when I was very young, and there was no communication between us about my birth mother. I learned the lesson well that I was to bury significant questions and related feelings.

This mode of being in the world without being deeply in touch with my feelings and without the freedom and encouragement to share intimately from my depths were inhibiting factors in my openness to God. To grow into the realization of the nature of God as revealed in Psalm 139 as the One who loves and knows, and as revealed in the caring of Jesus for little children, was to apprehend a radically different world than the one I was born into.

As in many families of that time, there were also to be no expressions of anger by the children and no questions or curiosity about sex. My stepmother would ask me to tie her corsets or wash her back when she took a bath, but in that prudish, Puritanical atmosphere I was to have no sexual feelings, thoughts, or fantasies. There was sexual stimulation and prohibition at the same time. The one overt piece of sex education was a book by a medical doctor which my stepmother gave me in early adolescence, in which the major teaching I remember was, "Masturbation will drive you to insanity." In relation to money, I was dutifully to keep in a little notebook an account of how I spent every penny of my small allowance. In the midst of this repression, conformity, and compliance, I just did not understand how my sister could break so many of the rules and still have the permissive love of my father. My journey to experiencing the love and grace of God as fundamental to the core of reality has been long and at times arduous. To believe that God willed my freedom and not my repression and compliance has been a huge leap of faith.

Blame

My father transferred his sorrow and guilt over my birth mother's death onto me in ways that were covert and passively punishing. My connection to my only living parent in childhood was so distant that a few years ago my sister said to me, "It was like your father was your stepfather, and your stepmother was your mother."

It has been fascinating to come to understand my internal bond with my father. Being ashamed, feeling inadequate, wrestling with guilt, being afraid of criticism and judgment have all kept me connected to that familiar image of my father in my mind. To be able to move beyond the voice of blame and criticism has required the faith and courage to stand without him, and to trust myself and my relationship with my heavenly Father.

Smother Love

While my stepmother's love was responsible for my very survival, it was also a controlling love that exacted a price: relinquishing some of my emotional freedom. When, during my first experience in therapy in my late twenties, I told my stepmother about my struggle to feel that it was safe to express my independence and to be assertive in my relationship with her, she was deeply wounded. After a couple of attempts at caringly communicating the trap I felt I was in as a child, to which she responded with the same pattern of "how could you say that" and "how could you do that to me," I resigned myself to relating to her in less emotional depth for the rest of my life.

But this meant that I have had to struggle to deepen my relationship with God amid the fear of losing my freedom and identity. Merton's explanation of the idea that the identity of God calls forth the true identity of the individual was comforting and liberating: "We are fulfilled by an identity that does not annihilate our own, which is ours, and yet is 'received.' It is a Person eternally other than ourselves who identifies Himself perfectly with ourselves. This Identity is Christ, God."[1] It has been a long journey to trust that intimacy with God is not engulfment, enmeshment, and neurotic control. My journal has accounts of those moments when I have encountered the relieving truth that my projections onto God—that God was hypersensitive and would reject me if I asserted my strength, independence, and aggression—were erroneous. "Thank you, God, for not being narcissistic and oversensitive, for not being a moody victim if I didn't do or say exactly the right thing, and for not abandoning me when I assert my freedom and independence. Thank you for your constancy and for your love, from which nothing in all creation can separate me, not even death. Thank you for your love, which will never let me go." This struggle finally led me to the transforming belief that the will of God was for me to wrestle with the will of God.

Wrestling with the Will of God[2]

Interpersonal patterns of passive compliance learned in our families of origin, perhaps reinforced by the church and school, are often seen as guiding principles of prayer. We think of submission rather than assertiveness as the will of God for the prayerful state. We see the throne of grace as approachable only with the submissive, passive side of ourselves. We think the gentle and receptive side of personality is acceptable for prayer, but assertiveness is taboo. We believe we should be obedient in a passive, compliant way to the will of God, and we are not aware of God's call and invitation to be obedient to God's will by wrestling with that will. The need to assert vigorously the depth and breadth of one's authentic self with all the relevant emotions and human needs is too frequently deemed unacceptable in communication with God. Our expressions of assertiveness and autonomous striving we suppress or repress.

When a child's feelings and needs have been squelched and her assertiveness has been labeled bad or sinful, then she may have difficulty perceiving God's gracious acceptance of her whole person. Such people often grow up believing that God can only care for the pious façade, the "good me," and that the "bad me" and the "not me" (the parts of ourselves that we hide even from ourselves) are totally unacceptable to God. Being "nice" or "good" are conditions we have to meet in order to persuade God to approve of us.

Passive submissiveness and the sacrifice of the authentic self are not the will of God, however. God is saddened that we believe we must destroy divinely given dimensions of our personalities in order to be loved. God caringly struggles on our behalf to lead us into that free space of joyous autonomy, where we live by trust in God's love and grace. God lovingly struggles on our behalf to help us find our individuality and express our unique autonomy. The Creator deeply desires that we, as God's children, experience the divine love that calls us into the freedom to be our whole selves. God's love calls forth our strength, our individuality, and our autonomy. God loves us wholly; God rejoices in our freedom; God celebrates our emerging autonomy; God validates our individuality. God knows that we do not feel truly accepted until all that is in us, including the "bad me" and the "not me," is experienced as accepted by God.

Some of us have experienced this affirmation of our autonomy and assertiveness on the human interpersonal level, but we may not have transferred that learning to our relationship to God. The relationship of parents to children may help to clarify this point. Parents often delight in seeing their children move into and through the various developmental stages of human growth and toward individuality. There is joy over the first word spoken or over new phrases that are articulated, and parental "oohs and ahs" resound over a baby's first steps. Parents can offer a variety of affirming expressions for the growth and development of a child's personality and individuality. Many parents are enthusiastic about their children's unfolding personhood. How much more does the divine Parent celebrate our steps into our freedom and autonomy as God's beloved children.

In spiritual direction or counseling, the director or therapist will often feel aligned with the part of the counselee that is struggling for the freedom to be, even before the counselee can fully claim that desire for his own life. The counselor is concerned for the individual's fullest expression of personhood and for the unfolding of the image of God in the counselee. How much more is God's love involved in the struggle for our autonomy and individuality! If we can experience such an affirmation for others' autonomy in our caring, so much more does God's love seek to validate our unique personhood.

This does not mean God blesses a new kind of narcissism in terms of idolatrous self-actualization. God does not place a benediction on the self-actualizing person who puts herself at the center of the world without reference to the Creator and to bringing love and justice to the neighbor. Personal growth and development do not mean we are the savior or messiah for ourselves. God does not place a benediction on a psychological or spiritual hedonism that says, "You do your own thing, and I'll do mine." That is not the gospel. Rather, God affirms the depth of individual personhood in the context of our relationship to God and in terms of love and justice with our neighbors. In fact, the deepest acceptance of our own individuality and autonomy can be experienced only through the knowledge that the ultimate Source of Being is also the Divine Affirmer and Guarantor of indestructible identity.

Although devotional literature dealing with the theme of assertiveness and autonomy in prayer is sparse, in a little-known book titled *The Soul of Prayer*, Peter Taylor Forsyth devotes the last chapter to the subject of the insistency of prayer.[3] Emphasizing the importunity of prayer, Forsyth maintains that it is the will of God for people to wrestle with God in prayer out of their strength as well as their weakness. He is critical of the popular theme that acquiescence, submissiveness, and passivity should be dominant in the life of prayer. He points out that the phrase "Thy will be done" appropriately reflects an attitude of submissiveness only after an assertive struggle, such as Jesus had in the Garden of Gethsemane. Jesus initially prayed that the cup of suffering might be removed from his lips, and it was then and only then that Jesus said, "Nevertheless, not my will, but thine, be done."[4]

There is much biblical support for the view that God wants an interactive encounter with us in prayer, and that we are to address God out of our strength and our assertiveness, and not simply out of our submissiveness or weakness. Jesus encourages seeking, knocking, and asking. There is the parable of the unjust judge, who responds finally to the request of the importunate widow. There is the incident of the Syrophoenician woman, who encountered Jesus forcefully and apparently changed his intention by the manner of her approach. The struggling cries of the psalmist, the confessions of Jeremiah, and the protestations of Job are but a few Old Testament examples of bringing assertiveness and strength into the life of prayer.

Jacob wrestling with an angel of God is a helpful paradigm for this theme of God's desire to engage people in strenuous and vigorous encounter. Divine love and caring initiated the wrestling, not to oppose Jacob, but to enable Jacob to discover his true identity and then his mission in life. God was not simply there to celebrate the gift of identity that Jacob wrestled out of his experience. Rather, God was present to help Jacob begin the struggle to discover his true identity and affirm his uniqueness, autonomy, and freedom to be.

Wrestling with God in prayer in a strenuous and vigorous way is not done in the spirit of competitiveness or as antagonists. Rather, the wrestling can be compared to the passionate embracing of two lovers who seek to affirm each other in sharing their love. God is an assertive and affirming God of love, initiating for our own good the struggle for the freedom of our personhood and our individuality. As we experience God's nature in that lovingly vigorous and dynamic way, we may discover that God is calling forth in us that same kind of vigor, strength, and assertiveness of our total beings in order to fulfill our lives.

A prayer that summarizes this theme of assertiveness and autonomy in prayer might contain the following thoughts and feelings: "O God, who is divine love, inviting forth all the potential in us, how great you are. Your loving strength initiates and calls forth the freedom in us to be ourselves, even when we doubt that it is all right to assert our needs and our feelings. We are grateful that you are not a fragile or a touchy God who cannot accept us and relate to us out of our strengths. We are grateful that you seek us out that we may be fully human and experience the widest spectrum of our feelings. Enable us to bring all of ourselves to you, that we may know the full acceptance of your love, and that we may exercise the depth of our powers in your loving service. Amen."

God is ever seeking to bring us into life by inviting us with all our strengths, assertiveness, individuality, and total personhood into loving and prayerful encounter with divine love. We could speak of ministry, especially of counseling and spiritual direction, as a crusade to free people from the demonic and self-destructive patterns of their existence so that the authentic image of God that is buried in each person can be free to live, love, have meaning, and be in intimate relationship and dialogue with God. A part of that ministry is to help people become free from their fixation on false absolutes and their idolatrous prayers to those idols. It seeks to enable persons to live in the new reality, the new creation, where their communication with God is freeing, liberating, loving, and justice seeking.

The Push into the Unbearable: My Mother's Death

As God can use even pharaohs for the disclosure of God's purposes and nature, so it was that God used my clinical work with severely disturbed people to open up my tissue memory of the chaos of the first five and a half weeks of my life and the terrible separation anxiety in relationship to my mother's death. My clients pushed me to be responsible for their life and death (as I was for both my mother and stepmother). They demanded that I give more and more and prove more and more my caring, but there was never enough proof for them. They reached into the depth of my psyche to challenge me to face my deepest wound, my unhealed center and my emotional Achilles' heel through their inordinate demands, their murderous rage, their despair, and their challenge that if I truly loved them I would save them.

I had to face the humiliating fact that too often I was taking care of other people and infantilizing them because I was so frightened of being responsible if their lives did not turn out all right—if they killed themselves. I had to confront a huge error in my thinking: that I was omnipotent and was their savior and redeemer. I tried to be for them what I yearned to have for myself—the ideal mother. I tried to heal their overwhelming fears of abandonment because I could not bear the anxiety of my own abandonment as an infant. Had it not been for the incredible push by these difficult clients and the firm, supportive insistence of my caring wife and a deeply thoughtful psychiatric consultant, I might have never realized that separation anxiety was the dominant power in my life rather than love and grace. So I was forced to struggle with my need for the undying love of an eternal Parent.

Object Constancy and the Eternal Presence of God

The human heart yearns to know the constancy of love. The developing child needs to know the presence of a familiar love that it can trust to be there. The dependent infant needs to know that there is a love that will respond to its needs and reliably cherish, take care of, mirror, echo, affirm, validate, and truly know. The child needs to experience that there is a love beyond itself that truly has empathy for and understanding of the inner essence of the child. In psychological terms, the child needs "object constancy." In spiritual terms, everyone needs an everlasting love.

Psychologists Charles Cohen and Vance Sherwood believe that object constancy is a critical organizing factor in personality. This object constancy involves a child's having repeated and successful experiences of being separated from and reunited with the mother. Employing the game of peek-a-boo as a metaphor, Cohen and Sherwood define object constancy as

> the sense that the mother is constantly available in her mirroring function. Children who feel that the mother who sees them is always available may pursue independent functioning with security. By contrast, children who lack the sense that the mirroring mother is constantly available will have trouble becoming their own persons, and will be forced to build their own identities upon staying close. If the child needs the mother to feel safe, and if the mother cannot be counted on to be available when the child moves off, then the child will not

move off. Clinging dependency replaces object constancy as the chief source of security, and identity must then be built around having some other who offers definition, not around the pursuit of the child's own intentions and initiatives.[5]

We can relate this need for object constancy in the infant-mother relationship to the client-therapist or directee-director relationship and to the individual-God relationship. Each person has an innate need for the Divine Parent or Divine Mother to be an object of constancy that can be counted on even when the person wanders into a far country. But we tend to project or transfer automatically to the Godhead any lack of human object constancy we experience in our early years. Oftentimes people who have a lot of insecurity about the staying power of significant people in their lives unconsciously choose love partners who will continue to provoke the threat of rejection and abandonment. Their choice of a field of work or work situation sometimes recreates that same fear of disapproval, loss, and rejection.

The ability to introject—to incorporate or internalize—a loving, soothing, and mirroring object appears to be essential for mental and spiritual health. It also seems to be necessary for us to experience the Basic Object (God) of the cosmos as the kind of loving, mirroring, and validating presence that we can trust when we go off in some independent or even rebellious and angry direction. We need to be able to trust that the Ultimate Power of the universe is not fickle, whimsical, or narcissistically oversensitive, but rather that God functions with an undying love, an everlasting faithfulness, and endless devotion. Julian of Norwich spoke of this experience of the relationship with God as being "endlessly loved with an endless love."[6]

Psalm 139 is a wonderful illustration of the object constancy of the Divine. The Loving God knows us in our mother's womb, and that Creator God remains the Knowing Love or the Loving

Knower for the rest of our lives. That knowing is like the mirroring, echoing, affirming, and validating love that psychologists speak of as being necessary for all children if they are to develop in an emotionally healthy manner.

Object Constancy and Death

Object constancy has been an elusive experience for me for much of my life. And I have always feared the lack of such loving connection through my death. Anticipating death, for those who lost their mother in infancy, may be terrifying because they project the loss of the mother at birth into a potential repetition of losing God—at death. Such people may ask if God's caring is like that of the deceased mother, a "dying love." Or can we trust, as Romans 8 suggests, in God's "undying love" because nothing can separate us from the love of God in Christ Jesus? But such wounded people may be afraid of the hell of isolation and abandonment, just as it happened as they came into the world. They may ask along with me, Why won't the same thing happen when I leave this world? Why isn't the exit the same as the entrance? I lived much of my life terrified of abandonment and rejection since that happened to me at the beginning of life when I was most vulnerable. I have worked very hard since then to make sure that other people would not reject me. I have worked diligently to make sure that God would not be displeased with me and send me to hell for all time—the ultimate disapproval—where I would be isolated and alone forever. Since I do not know or trust the object constancy of the God of grace and love and I project that God's attitude is one of condemnation and rejection, I live in fear for the end of my life as another trauma of abandonment.

Self-Atonement Strategies

My survival involved some defensive strategies which also became self-atonement behaviors. There were three factors in my separation anxiety: (1) the death of and the resulting abandonment by my birth mother, which left terror in the marrow of my bones and in my tissue memory, though quite unconscious; (2) my father's rejection of me as the cause of my mother's death and his detachment and emotional distance from me; (3) my fear that I would do emotional injury to my stepmother, and that she, who was really my major source of nurture and thus my lifeline, would somehow be overwhelmed and leave me to be orphaned.

My atonement strategies were built upon keen emotional radar (later put to good use, I hope, as a pastoral counselor) that was tuned in to what my stepmother and father needed and wanted so that I could be sure of a place to survive and belong. People pleasing was the name of the game. In addition, achievements that they could be happy with and proud of were important means to attain and retain love. I was adept at participating in the family conspiracy of silence and the repression and avoidance of key issues, questions, and emotions. I crucified various dimensions of my personality in order to survive, gain approval, and try to merit God's acceptance (or at least avoid hell). My world had to depend on me, and with secret resentment in my heart for sacrificing my real self, I carried out my loving ministry to others. While I preached, taught, and counseled about the love and grace of God for others, I found that the lens through which I saw the world in the context of my family of origin made it very difficult for me to trust that God in Christ was the Supreme Love and Rescuing Savior.

Questions for Personal Reflection

1. Are there any themes in your life that have created pain or caused you to struggle in order to trust that God's love and grace are foundational and constant for you?

2. Are there any relationships, losses, and fears that have made it difficult for you to understand the nature of the Divine

Parent as being quite different from the problematic relationships of your childhood?

3. Can you describe the various relationships with authority that have defined who you are or have been? Can you presently experience yourself as answering the question, Whose are you? in relation to your being the beloved and cherished child of God?

4. Can you write a prayer that reflects your thankfulness for belonging fundamentally to the God of love as revealed in Jesus Christ?

UNDERSTANDING YOUR FAMILY OF ORIGIN

▲▲▲▲▲▲▲▲▲▲

Communication Patterns with Family and with God

The basic forms, values, injunctions against, and permission for communication develop in your family of origin. The authorities inside the family generally teach their children about communication (sometimes reinforced and occasionally challenged by schoolteachers, clergy, pediatricians, etc.). These fundamental patterns tend to persist throughout your life, and they generally are transferred to your modes of communication with God. The basic rules and dynamics of interactive communication in the family of origin usually set the tone for your life of prayer and interactions with God. For example, if a child grows up in an alcoholic family with the three basic rules that Claudia Black has indicated—(1) don't feel, (2) don't share, and (3) don't trust[1]— then that child will generally have difficulty with being transparent, open, and vulnerable with God.

As an evolving spiritual person you need to become aware of, and to take responsibility for, the patterns, defenses, inhibitions, injunctions, and rules concerning communication in your family of origin so that you may have the inner freedom to choose for yourself how you seek to relate creatively to the Divine Parent. Spiritual growth requires moving from an unconscious and unaware mindset about your communication values and patterns to a conscious and responsible understanding about your communication style. Hellmuth Kaiser even posited that duplicity in communication is the "Universal Symptom" of psychopathology and that healing takes place through genuine and honest communication.[2]

Let us explore some basic communication issues that often need transformation in order for the seeker to move more deeply into union, communion, and conversation with the Divine.

Blame

Some years ago, Eric Berne suggested that the favorite psychological game in America was the blame game, "If It Weren't for You." That game began with Adam, who passed the original buck in blaming both God and Eve for his disobedience: "The woman whom thou gavest to be with me, she gave me the fruit of the tree, and I ate."[3]

This copping out from taking responsibility for self has become a major ingredient in dysfunctional marriages and families in which someone else is always at fault. In this blame context people usually focus on blaming others for their own unhappiness. Instead of an open and vulnerable "I feel" statement, there is a "You are wrong and bad" statement, usually with an implicit or explicit character assassination element involved, such as "You're stupid," or "You're a jerk." In an age of victimization and trivial litigation over such things as hot coffee cups, people are prone to avoid looking at their own responsibilities and deep feelings, and to blame someone else for their difficulties. Such scapegoating of other people and organizations is often linked to the pattern of blaming God when things don't go the way we want them to go. We must distinguish between a healthy, mature, empowered, and responsible prophetic call for social justice, and a whining, manipulative, blaming approach to relationships. Such narcissistic, self-centered, destructive entitlement claims in the blame game are a playing out of Jesus' concern about our being so focused on the splinter in someone else's eye that we miss the log in our own eye.

Emotional Reactivity

Closely linked to blame is emotional reactivity, which Edwin Friedman and Murray Bowen highlighted in their family systems work.[4] Reactivity refers to an impulsive reaction to stressful and hurtful situations. People with a high degree of emotional reactivity have knee-jerk reactions to various events, situations, comments, and behaviors of others. They have no inner freedom to choose their response. They are usually unaware that they give away their power to other people or to external situations, and their defensive reactions generally mask their vulnerability, hurt, and helplessness. But on the surface the emotionally reactive person appears to be strong and in control, through displaying anger or using a punishing silent treatment.

Albert Ellis and other therapists have suggested an ABC for understanding emotional reactivity, in which one's emotional hot buttons are pushed, and the individual reacts automatically and defensively without thinking. In this formulation,

> A stands for the *activating* event or the upsetting cause.
>
> B stands for the *belief* or imputed meaning an individual gives to the activating event or upsetting situation; this projected belief about or interpretative meaning for the event is outside of one's awareness.
>
> C stands for the *consequence* or the emotional reaction to the activating event.[5]

Most people tend to move from A to C without ever stopping at or becoming aware of B. That is, people generally are not aware that there is a rapid thought process that involves a quick interpretation of the meaning of the activating event. Thus, people give up their freedom to choose how to respond, rather than to react, to those situations and persons which press their emotional hot buttons.

Stephen Covey has highlighted the importance of our being free to move from a position of emotional reactivity to a position of mature proactivity, which

> means that as human beings, we are responsible for our own lives. Look at the word responsibility—"response-ability"—the ability to choose your response. Highly proactive people recognize that responsibility. They do not blame circumstances, conditions, or conditioning for their behavior. Their behavior is a product of their own conscious choice, based on values, rather than a product of their conditions, based on feeling.[6]

To enable us to find the inner emotional space to choose our response rather than to react impulsively, we can listen to our breathing, count to ten, pray, or use some other relaxation method. It is important for us to reclaim our power over our own hot buttons and to establish the freedom for our executive or adult ego, linked with the spirit of love, to function proactively in difficult situations.

Other Communication Defenses:
Silent Treatment, Porcupine Quills,
Somaticization, and Acting Out

Families, as well as others, teach us or model for us various ways to protect ourselves from feeling our true emotions and from articulating those feelings, needs, and thoughts genuinely to others. These protective strategies often get transferred into our communication patterns with Ultimate Reality as well. Behind these protective patterns are usually feelings of inadequacy, fear, hurt, guilt, helplessness, grief, and the like. People act invulnerable in order to protect their vulnerability. We often don't trust ourselves with naming and speaking the truth of what we feel and think, nor do we trust others to receive our vulnerable communications with tender acceptance and loving understanding.

In some families, one or more authority figures model the defensive use of the silent treatment as a way of dealing with hurt, disappointment, and conflict. These people withdraw from open communication and utilize their considerable manipulative power of moody silence to punish others for their "unforgivable sins" of omission or commission. "I'll never speak to him (or her) again" is a major pattern in some families for generations in dealing with hurt, differences, and discord. In some families, the person employing the silent treatment carries a phony aura of spiritual blessedness as a martyr or victim. But, as Everett Shostrom, a California psychologist with spiritual interests, has shown from his research on manipulative people, the sulking martyr and moody victim wield great power in a family, and sometimes in an organizational system.[7] ("If I don't get my way, I'll leave the church and take my stewardship pledge with me.") Thus, the apparent underdog often outmaneuvers the others in a system and holds the final power, sometimes by playing on the guilt feelings of others. This controlling silence that blocks communication, punishes the other, and bars the way to forgiveness and mutual reconciliation is quite contrary to the admonition of Jesus, who asks that we reconcile and make peace with our brothers and sisters before we come with a gift to the altar. In this pattern, the martyr assumes the role of the ultimate judge with the power to punish and condemn those who do not perform according to the expectations of the so-called victim, who is really functioning as a passive-aggressive victimizer.

Don Williamson, a family therapist, has a delightful technique for trying to keep your own proactive power when dealing with such a pouting martyr. He suggests that you find adult phrases that name the truth of the situation in a positive and constructive manner. Your statement should also indicate that you are not controlled by the sulker. For example, the patriarchal grandfather of a family started to pout over the fact that his adult son and his family could not come to see him for their usual Thanksgiving visit because their daughter was playing in the high school band for the Thanksgiving Day football game. On the phone, the adult son said to his father, "We all love you, and be assured that if we were able to visit any patriarch on Thanksgiving Day, it would be with you."[8]

The defensive maneuver we call "flight or fight" response can cause us to use protective devices such as anger, criticism, and "porcupine quills" to keep others under control. Defensive people tend to dominate relationships through the power play of anger or the threat of anger. They try to control decision making and the expression of ideas, feelings, and needs through dictatorial and bullying tactics. They maintain their invulnerability by expressing intimidating anger. They often get involved in dirty fighting, such as attacking the very worth and identity of other people. Looking deeper, we find that such argumentative and dominating people are usually trying to protect their soft emotional underbellies, much as the porcupine uses its quills to protect its tender underside. These people usually struggle to hide their sensitivity, hurt, disappointment, sadness, fear, insecurity, inadequacy, and the like. They are similar to counterdependent people, who hide their vulnerability and dependency needs behind the protective strength of defensive hyperindependence.

Adult children of such defensive parents need to connect (often only in imagination) with the vulnerable inner child of the parent. By doing this, they may be able to demythologize the powerful, controlling parent, and humanize him by that process.

It may also free the adult child from imitating, often unconsciously, the defensive fighting style of the parent. Too often, such people believe that there are only two roles in life: the oppressor and the oppressed. With that limited choice in mind, some children grow up determined not to "roll over and play dead like my mom did with my dad." Thus, they identify with the aggressor and repress the tender core of feelings, which are so important in developing an authentic spiritual life. In the spiritual journey, we need to begin to find relationships of trust with people and the Divine so we can disclose to ourselves and to others the true nature of the underlying feelings and needs that we experience.

Another defensive strategy used to avoid speaking the truth in love is somaticization, which means placing emotional truth into the body itself. As we better understand the interaction of the mind, body, and spirit, we are becoming aware that many unexpressed feelings get channeled through the body. Research has shown that stifled grief and repressed anger provide at least the seedbed for some ailments. It is as if the very being of a person cries out to express the inner truth, and if it is not safe to do so in words, then the mind will choose a particular organ or a specific illness in which to express the repressed truth. Unfortunately, there is often a high price to pay for the body's articulation of the hidden truth. If you were punished in childhood for seeking to express your point of view, you may be punished later by pain, surgery, and suffering for the body's attempt to speak the unspeakable. So listen to the language of the body to see if it is seeking to help you articulate the repressed truth. It is also important to explore whether a "second-chance family" of relationships among friends, in a congregation, or with a counselor or a spiritual mentor can provide a safe and accepting environment for expressing your truth without having to pay the penalty of bodily sickness or frequent accidents.

Another style of defensive communication is acting out, or

putting the emotional truth into external behavior, instead of verbally articulating the inherent messages involved. When a family does not allow a member to articulate so-called "negative" feelings, that person may express those unacceptable thoughts and feelings in behaviors that will hurt the ones who have been controlling in some way. For example, a spouse who is unfaithful may be communicating hurt, disappointment, and anger that have not been verbally shared in mutually acceptable ways in the marital relationship. A youth who feels squelched may function as "the street devil and the house angel." A parishioner whose child or spouse dies may withdraw from the church and have nothing to do with religion anymore. The behavior is the message, and the recipient of the message usually experiences the hostile meaning inherent in the acting-out behavior. An extreme example of this was a female client who contemplated suicide as a way to express her hurt, emotional pain, and anger at family members who neglected, ignored, or openly rejected her. She imagined how they would pass by her open casket and feel terrible about how they had mistreated her. She expressed some glee at their potential guilt and emotional pain. I pointed out, "As you know, you won't really be there to enjoy their remorse." The shock of that reality caused her to reconsider putting her hurt and anger into suicidal behavior.

People often act out against God without articulating their needs, thoughts, and feelings directly to the Divine. People may avoid honest dialogue with Eternal Love because they do not believe that God cares, listens, or responds, just as the "loved ones" in the family of origin did not respond constructively to them.

In the communication process, we must remember that people see others and events in various ways. It is not uncommon in a family, for example, for siblings to perceive their parents somewhat differently. Some go so far as to say that siblings in the same family do not have the same emotional parents because of birth order, family conditions, or differences in personality in each sibling. In couple relationships, it is often said that there are six different selves interacting. For example, in a marriage, the six selves are: the wife as she really is, the husband's image of her, and her own self-image; the husband as he really is, his wife's image of him, and his own self-image. We are always communicating with people as we imagine them to be. Dr. Dorsey, a psychiatrist at Wayne State University many years ago, would always refer to people as "my President Kennedy," "my Katherine Hepburn," and so on, in order to clearly distinguish his perception of that person from the real person. A cartoon from the book *A Child's Guide to Freud* shows a boy, who is upset with his father, drawing a picture on newsprint of his father as a dragon, with the caption, "My father is a dragon." When he takes his picture over to his father, and the father puts his head through the dragon portrait, it is clear that the real father is not a dragon.[9]

In a similar way, our perceptions of God may be skewed. As Robert Llewellyn wrote: "But prayer becomes true only as the distortions affecting our image of God are corrected."[10] To be able to communicate as much as possible from one's own real self to the true self of another is important.

People have a tender, vulnerable core of genuine feelings which is at the emotional center of their lives. Too often, their defensive styles of communication or their misperceptions of others and of themselves function as barriers to open and authentic communication.

Interaction often involves the defensive styles of each person and their misperceptions of one another and of self. Too little communication takes place directly between the tender, vulnerable core of each party. Likewise, people may transfer these patterns and erroneous images to the relationship with the Divine so that no genuine communication can take place. C. S. Lewis showed an appreciation of this dilemma of the human-divine interaction in his saying, "May it be the real Thou that I speak to; may it be the real me who speaks."

In the tender, vulnerable core, numerous authentic feelings may be utilized in growing spiritually in relationship to God, others, and self, such as hurt, fear, anger, guilt, and love.

Hurt is the first emotion to focus on, and this includes a sense of disappointment, sadness, loss, and grief. These feelings are a natural part of any close, interpersonal relationship. It has been said that grief is love's way of saying goodbye to those for whom we have cared. In addition, when we do love other people, we are also vulnerable to being disappointed and hurt by them. We have many ways of protecting and defending ourselves against such vulnerability, disappointment, and hurt.

Reflect for a moment on your ways of dealing with your hurt when a loved one disappoints you. Which of the defensive styles of communication might you utilize as a way of protecting your vulnerability? Perhaps you might mask your hurt by sulking and withdrawing, possibly with a silent treatment designed to get revenge on the one who hurt you. Or perhaps you might directly retaliate and attack the one who has disappointed you with anger, criticism, or blame, in order to avoid your hurt feelings as well as to hurt the one who hurt you. Sometimes people take their hurt feelings inside themselves and become depressed, or turn the emotion of sadness into somatic symptoms. How difficult it often is to identify hurt for what it is, and to express it cleanly and directly, instead of converting it into some other expression or reaction. To communicate sadness as sadness, or hurt as hurt, rather than concealing it, is a major step psychologically and spiritually, in developing mature communication patterns.

During the past few decades, psychology has rediscovered the truth of Jesus' statement, "Blessed are they that mourn: for they shall be comforted."[11] Owning and expressing hurt and grief directly offer opportunity for constructive communication that may lead to comfort, healing, and reconciliation in relationships. For those whose dynamics require them to be in control, invulnerable, and defensively strong, it may be hard to be open to the experience and expression of sad and hurt feelings. Yet, research indicates that emotional and physical health are better served by following the sound principle in Jesus' words about mourning in the service of healing and comfort.

The rules and principles, usually from the family of origin, that govern our identification and expression of sadness and disappointment are generally transferred to our interaction with God, so that if there has been repression and denial of grief in our human encounters, we often will hide and mask our sadness in our interactions with God in prayer. Let me add a note of caution about the manipulative use of hurt feelings by martyrs who tweak the guilt of others in order to get their own way. These people play what Eric Berne called the immature game of "poor, rejected me," a perversion of the genuine expression of grief and hurt.

Fear includes the experiences of feeling frightened, insecure, helpless, and inadequate. Men, in particular, have been taught by families and society that they should not disclose this part of themselves because these experiences of fear, insecurity, and inadequacy are unmasculine and weak. Thus people may act like the invulnerable Rock of Gibraltar on the outside, when they really feel frightened and alone on the inside. Oftentimes, fear is masked by the defense of blame and anger in interpersonal relationships. People may stake out the overcompensatory position of being right, secure, and strong in order to cover the fearful and insecure part of their lives. This defensive posture against revealing one's inadequacies is reminiscent of the preacher who wrote himself a note in the margin of his sermon manuscript: "Weak point. Pound pulpit harder." It often takes a lot of courage for people to face honestly their fears, inadequacies, and experience of helplessness during life's difficult happenings. However, disclosing your fears and insecurities within intimate relationships, and finding them accepted and not ridiculed, may provide a profound experience that deepens the bonds of love. Likewise, accepting the insecurities and fears of people in your intimate circle can bring you deep rewards in those interpersonal relationships. Certainly, your prayer life is affected by the way your history has valued insecurity and fear and the expressions of those feelings. The goal is to transcend any oppressive rules and principles that would keep you from sharing the depth of your heart with God about your own terrors and inadequacies.

Anger, for many spiritual people, is one of the most difficult emotions to deal with constructively in either human relationships or in relationship to the Divine. Too often, anger has been polluted with repressive injunctions from the family of origin, masquerading as religious truths. "Be not angry" may be the distorted family interpretation of the biblical directive, "Be angry but do not sin,"[12] that has formed a person's belief system concerning anger. Too often, people have not had sound guidelines for learning how to express anger constructively. They may have learned repressive injunctions against expressing any anger, or they may have had impulsive rage and violence modeled for them. Simply pushing anger down inside, where it may fester into an emotional gunnysack of resentment, is potentially as destructive as the anger that flails wildly in words and actions at anyone who is within reach. William Blake expressed the basic principle of the appropriate handling and discharge of anger in his poem "A Poison Tree":

> . . . I was angry with my friend;
> I told my wrath, my wrath did end.
> I was angry with my foe;
> I told it not, my wrath did grow.

Finding appropriate outlets for anger and creatively discharging it in words, actions, and fantasies are important steps in developing constructive relationships. Biblically, we have the examples of people like Job, Jeremiah, and the psalmist, who vented their wrath at God; they somehow felt secure enough to challenge their Maker.

In recent years, some therapists have suggested that much

anger is caused by the absolutist demands that we place on others to behave exactly according to our prescribed, and sometimes arrogant and perfectionistic, expectations. They have rediscovered what François Fenelon spoke of centuries ago, that "anger is the daughter of pride."[13] The implicit theme of the self-righteous, angry person with significant others may be, "I am angry with you because you are not what I want you to be. You must be and do what I want, or I will remain justifiably angry with you until you change your behavior to conform to my expectations." Instead of focusing our self-justifying anger on the imperfections and the bad behavior of others, we may need to look inward to challenge our own "shoulds" and "musts" that insist that others must be and do what we arrogantly demand. Challenging our own assumptions about how other people should be may offer a significant step in the transformation of our anger-creating belief system.

Anger can be used to defend against a lot of other emotions. For example, when people feel afraid, inadequate, insecure, sad, or helpless, they may mask their vulnerability by showing anger. The person who uses anger to avoid experiencing and expressing the emotional truths of these other feelings needs to find courage and a safe relationship in which to identify and express the underlying emotions. So often in interpersonal relationships, an angry person who feels helpless, sad, and powerless to do anything about the other person's attitude or behavior nonetheless keeps trying aggressively to change the other person. This defensively angry person is giving away power to the other and implicitly communicating, "I cannot really be okay and feel secure until you stop acting as you do. I do not have control over my own emotional life, and I can only be reactive to you. Therefore, you must change, so I can regain my own self-control and emotional security."

Guilt has various connotations for different folk. Some people in the field of mental health label all guilt as bad, since they experience so many of their clients as having been emotionally distraught and injured by authorities who induced guilt and shame. However, others say that we need to distinguish false, unhealthy, and immature guilt from a healthy sense of mature, responsible, and true guilt that can be utilized for growth and development, both emotionally and spiritually. False guilt can be attributed to those false authorities that function as if they had divine judgment and ultimate righteousness on their side, seeking to induce guilt in those around them in order to control them and their behavior. Such false and unhealthy guilt requires a challenge to the false authorities and a revolution by those who have been afflicted with it. On the other hand, true guilt is in the spirit of, "Against thee, thee only, have I sinned,"[14] in which we honestly acknowledge our failures and our shortcomings in relation to our Creator and Redeemer, and in which we ask for forgiveness and healing. Often when a person is able to take responsibility for his own behavior, with constructive guilt, then change and transformation can take place. The truth of confession and repentance and a turning away from the destructive patterns of the old self are often absolutely essential to the vitality and life of the new self that seeks to live in the new creation. For a good discussion of true and false guilt, see Paul Tournier's book, *Guilt and Grace*.[15] Guilt often is hidden by projecting blame on others, or by masking the guilt under some defensive maneuver of strength. Sometimes the guilt can go into the body so that a person incapacitates herself physically in some way, in order to provide her own punishment. People dealing with the complexities of guilt should be encouraged to be able to confess that guilt in the context of an understanding and accepting relationship. Guilt can be poisonous. We need forgiveness and grace to heal its damage.

Love would seem to be the easiest emotion to identify and to share, but it is surprising how often, even in so-called intimate relationships, caring, warmth, and tenderness are not communicated meaningfully, authentically, and directly. It is amazing to see how often couples who supposedly married for love have a distance in their intimate relationship, or actually feel hostile. Many of these people are afraid to show love because in their families of origin, they were emotionally injured by the people who were supposed to love them most. Abuse, trauma, neglect, and abandonment often were key factors in what should have been the primary love relationships in the family. These people are frightened of reaching out in vulnerable, caring ways for fear of being injured again. Erich Fromm has pointed out that while people are afraid of not being loved, the deeper and often more unconscious fear is the fear of loving.[16] A. H. Maslow and Bela Mittleman have defined love as "lowering one's defenses and becoming vulnerable to hurt."[17] This courage to love and to risk the possibility of being hurt is not to be misinterpreted as being masochistic, but as a healthy caring for others. When we reach out in love, even in marriage, the family, or in church, there is no guarantee that love will be returned. Loving is always a risk; love is an inward cross. Some people ask for a guarantee that their love will always be returned, and that they will never have to face what Jesus faced in his most intimate relationships with his disciples, the possibility of denial and betrayal. When we have been hurt and rejected too much in close relationships, we tend to build defenses to keep us safe from the involvements of loving, with the inherent possibilities of being hurt again. However, if we are to build constructive relationships throughout life, then we have to develop the courage to care and to reach out to others from our vulnerable centers of tenderness, accepting the possibility of conflict and hurt. For Christians, this pattern of caring is reflected in the gift to us of God's love in Jesus Christ, and even in the accompanying human rejections he suffered on the cross, over which Divine Love was ultimately triumphant. Certainly, the scriptures are very clear about God's initiatory love to us and God's invitation to us to respond in love to God, to others, and to the self.

To connect love, communication, and prayer, I know of no better way than to quote from David Jacobsen in his epilogue to *Clarity in Prayer:*[18]

Prayer is rooted in love.

The experience of prayer is the experience of love.

Prayer is the means by which we develop the intimacy with God which is love.

Prayer is love.

Love is prayer.

What we yearn for in life is the certainty that God is and that

God loves.

To know that with our minds or to hold that as a belief is important but not complete.

When we experience prayer, we experience that certainty.

The experience is movement toward completion of our knowing that certainty.

The more we experience the communication of prayer, the deeper is the sense of intimacy which comes.

Our "chief end" (that is, our primary purpose of life) is to "know God and to enjoy God forever." That is what the old catechism says.

We get to "know God" in prayer. Intimacy comes in that experience.

To "know God" is to enjoy God. To truly know God is to experience God's love.

God will love you if you never pray.

Prayer is the gift of grace which offers us an opportunity to develop intimacy with God. This intimacy is the experience of the love God has already given us. It is a high privilege.

Roots and Wings

Across the life span, people yearn to have a fundamental love relationship that will give them a sense of belonging and connectedness on the one hand, and on the other hand an affirmation of their independence and autonomy. The famous quotation about parenting children reflects this truth: "Wise parents can give children only two things: roots and wings." Adults seek in couple relationships to find someone who will love them in a similar way that affirms both the togetherness in the relationship and the freedom of each to be the unique self. In marriage, this process is sometimes described as moving though three stages of the love relationship:

1. The *We* stage, in which there is a romantic merging of two lives.
2. The struggle for an *I* in the relationship, which often brings tension.
3. The *We-I* stage, in which a couple has learned to balance togetherness and individuality.

The Stone Center group, which explores women's psychological development, refers to this loving polarity as "connected autonomy."[19] Others call it "intimate autonomy" and "autonomous intimacy." In relationship to the Divine, people yearn to experience that connectedness and communion with God, as well as to experience God's loving encouragement of their freedom to be themselves, each a particular child of God.

Children often feel forced to make a choice between the need for love (the roots of belonging and connection) and the need for freedom (the wings of autonomy and independence) in a relationship with a parent or parents. When children confront this dilemma, they face a fork in the emotional road: they must choose either love or freedom and give up the other.

Children who choose love and belonging sacrifice freedom and independence as the cost of maintaining the needed love relationship. Children who choose autonomy sacrifice the loving acceptance of a primary relationship. To choose love and connection alone leads to submission and adaptation; to choose freedom alone leads to opposition and rebellion. Paul Tournier notes how Jesus at the age of twelve, when he stayed behind in the Temple, did not choose either the "neurosis of submission" or the "neurosis of opposition."[20] Rather, Jesus noted that he must be about his heavenly Father's business, in which case he was not being either submissive or rebellious to his parents. Every human being needs to have the validation of the need for both roots and wings.

The life of one conservative Protestant female illustrates the dilemma of sacrificing independence for love. As a child, Sarah learned that her mother was hypersensitive to assertiveness or aggression by anyone in the family. Her mother would become deeply emotionally injured and fly into a blistering rage or retreat like a wounded deer if someone crossed her. Sarah's father was the extreme of the silent man, and so he modeled submissiveness and adaptation as the way of coping with life in general. The fundamentalist church also reinforced Sarah's belief system that it was evil, sinful, and harmful to be assertive. Sarah developed the life of a "neurotic saint," with the family's expectation of, the church's blessing for, and God's supposed benediction on her passivity. When Sarah became a minister, she was an extreme people pleaser and a do-gooder in her relationships. Sarah struggled for years to undo her idolatrous belief that it was "the will of God" for her to be passive, adaptive, and nonassertive. Sarah had great difficulty getting in touch with her hurt and her smoldering resentment that she had to repress a significant dimension of her personality in order to please her parents, her church, and her God. She had chosen love over freedom, and she came to realize that in her personal life and in her ministry, she needed both.

A major purpose of the family of origin and the healing ministries for those injured in that cauldron is to prepare people for both loving relationships and creative freedom. God really does seek to give us both roots and wings through healthy families and other revelations of divine love.

Your Spiritual Autobiography

Some people find it helpful to write an autobiography focusing on their growing-up years in their family of origin. You may want to use some of the ideas listed below as you develop your own creative way of writing your emotional and spiritual narrative based on your experiences with significant people in your childhood.

> You may situate yourself at one period of your childhood, or you may use a number of distinctive periods when there were significant changes within the family.
>
> Your autobiography may include descriptions of the characters in your history, the interactive patterns in those important relationships, photos, copies of actual letters received, time lines of significant events, drawings and diagrams of family patterns—whatever helps you understand your family history and your place in it.
>
> You may wish to highlight family relationships and experiences that have impacted your adult ways of relating to yourself, others, and God.
>
> You might describe the values, attitudes, beliefs, and any other positive or negative baggage that may influence your work or spiritual leadership role.
>
> You may wish to write three letters (not to be mailed, necessarily) to significant persons from childhood (living or deceased) with the purpose of sharing your emotional experience connected with those persons and the effects of each relationship on you. Try to write the letters from your tender, vulnerable core so that you

can share thoughts and feelings that may have been hidden in your heart for years. After completing those letters, try to imagine being in the inner world of each person receiving your letter. From each person's tender, vulnerable, and nondefensive core, try to write a thoughtful and sensitive response from that person to yourself. Sometimes this letter-writing exercise leads to a meaningful encounter between the hearts of two open and vulnerable persons.

You might find it helpful to think of such subjects as family rules, family myths, key family values, major family traditions (what did they mean and who upheld them?), spoken and unspoken expectations in your family, family strengths, the power structure in the family, how major family decisions were made, how disagreements and conflicts were managed, key illnesses or addictions, ethnic and cultural background, expressions of different emotions in the family, roles you played in the family, how the independence of children was encouraged or discouraged, your birth order, seminal events in the family, and the place of faith in the life of the family.

Genogram

You may wish to construct a genogram to lay out your intergenerational family history. I suggest that you look at the book *Genograms in Family Assessment*, by Monica McGoldrick and Randy Gerson,[21] or the videotape by the Menninger Foundation, *Constructing the Multi-Generational Genogram*,[22] for details on this process. You may find it valuable to trace key issues across at least three generations to see the impact of those patterns on you. For example, some of the patterns to consider are problems of addiction, abuse, and violence; skeletons in the closet; serious or chronic illnesses; suicides or suicide attempts; chronic emotional problems, including hospitalizations and medications; weight problems or eating disorders; extramarital relationships; separations and divorces; and religious affiliations and leadership roles.

You may wish to place images of God and beliefs about God in your genogram so you can readily see the various types of "household gods" that have been worshiped by your family over the years.

Conclusion

The goal of understanding various facets of your family history is to become better able to make conscious decisions about whether the beliefs, attitudes, and patterns of the past can be transformed for the future. May your prayer life reflect your asking for a deeper sense of the truth and reality of the gospel of love and grace, even though that may have been blurred and distorted by relationships and events of the past.

FACING THE LASTING EFFECTS FROM YOUR FAMILY OF ORIGIN

▲▲▲▲▲▲▲▲▲▲

It is well known that the rules, beliefs, and scripts that children learn in their family of origin tend to persist into adult life. Your worldview and your place in that childhood system usually become solidified in your psyche. It is generally not an easy process to become liberated and differentiated from internalized oppressive and neglectful authorities in your life. Likewise, it is often difficult to change your major role and style in relationships and to alter your key patterns of behavior. The process of becoming free from false absolutes (which is sometimes called demythologizing, de-absolutizing, and deterrorizing the idols) that have participated in developing your negative worldviews, distorted maps of reality, and erroneous beliefs about yourself and others is usually an enormous task. Your implicit spiritual drama that was formed out of your family experience tends to carry a dominating authority within it, as if it came directly from the hand of God rather than from the web of the relationships in your childhood family.

To help you reflect on some of the main issues that may have cemented you into certain patterns, I would like to introduce you to some new understandings of the lasting impact of your family of origin and some alternative approaches to providing healing for your soul, mind, and body from those dynamics.

The Trauma of Abuse

There is probably no deeper and longer lasting emotional effect upon children than that of the trauma of abuse that children suffer at the hands of those who are expected to love and to care for them. Many people on their spiritual journey are dealing with the terrible effects of physical, sexual, and emotional abuse. Abused children tend to be held in psychological and spiritual bondage by the horrors they have suffered. They often turn to the spiritual for healing; for example, certain seminaries have many students who were abused as children and who are seeking to recover from their abuse through their theological education. Abused children tend to develop a terrifying "trappedness" to the internalized abusive objects in the core of their being. They have great difficulty in detaching from those cruelly oppressive objects and attaching to reliable, trustworthy, and caring relationships. Only after enormous struggling can they become free of the connections to the abusive objects so that they can reorient their lives around the two commandments that involve loving relationships with God, others, and self.

Stephen Prior, a therapist in Boston who specializes in the treatment of sexually abused children, has suggested that four major factors constitute the psychological dynamics of such abused children.[1] Theologically, these four factors implicitly involve a distorted view of the world, of the self, and of ultimate reality.

1. *The relentless reliving of abusive relationships, either as victim or as perpetrator.*

It is well known that traumatized children tend to repeat abusive patterns of behavior in relationships, either as victim or as perpetrator, or in both roles at different times. For example, in adulthood these children often unconsciously choose partners who will be abusive to them. The familiar abusive objects are sought out as the objects of comfort. Also, parents who were abused as children may become abusive with their own children. Those who have been violated may also find ways to demean, attack, and abuse clergy, spiritual directors, and therapists.

In any event, the abused person is fundamentally closed off from redemptive, healing relationships of genuine love and caring by being fixated on the internalized abusive objects. There is a "relentless reliving of victim-victimizer experiences."

2. The reliance on identification with the aggressor as a basic mode of psychological defense.

Prior believes that because of "immense feelings of vulnerability," children use identification with the aggressor as an antidote to feeling afraid or weak, and they may use this identification to prevent perceived revictimization.

> This dynamic is particularly strong in boys who have been sexually abused by men. Boys typically reason unconsciously that if one is sexually assaulted by a man, then one must be a homosexual or a woman. Identification with the male aggressor is then needed as a defense not only against weakness and vulnerability in general, but against implicit feminization.

The dilemma for the child who identifies with the aggressor is that "the child may have the comforting illusion of being strong and powerful, but at the significant cost of being aggressive, violent and bad in his heart and actions." Such children, if they are enraged with their abusers, tend to attack and punish themselves for having identified with and acted like the abuser. From a spiritual point of view, such children seek to be their own savior from weakness and vulnerability by identifying with the aggressor, and then they judge and punish themselves by attacking the bad within. When a caring relationship appears in the intimate circle of the sexually abused child, the child wrestles with the terror of trust and of giving up the bad objects, and therefore, potential healers may be rejected and abused.

3. *The unshakable conviction of being the cause of the abuse, deserving the abuse, and being utterly bad.*

In a distortion of the doctrine of original sin, abused and neglected children often develop the conviction that their innate badness has caused the aggression, assaults, rejection, and abandonment that they receive. Such children develop an illusory omnipotence that they are in control of their world and that their behavior is what causes the traumatic things to happen to them. From this core of self-blame for being treated badly, such abused children may become adept at "getting therapists and even whole treatment systems to reject them."

In a psychological context, Prior uses the concept of possession, a term familiar in religious circles, to describe abused children's powerful sense of their ultimate badness. Many abused children develop a spontaneous conviction that they literally contain a "bad self" that can take possession of them and must be driven out or destroyed. They feel something akin to being possessed by the devil, and that somehow they must get rid of that core demon. "The abused person fears being abused again but also fears becoming an abuser. He fears that he will become like the abuser and traumatize the others. *This is the fear of possession by the bad object* [my emphasis]. Possession captures the abused child's belief—often all too accurate—that he will not simply act like his abuser but that he will become an abuser, that his entire personality will be taken over by a complete and fully-formed, evil identity."

A common symptom of traumatized children, Prior notes, is how with even the smallest upsetting event, they may suddenly become "possessed by intense, affectively charged models of interaction that they live out with drivenness and immense pain.

... They do not simply become angry or upset; they become possessed by terror and rage in quite frightening ways."

4. *The seeking of object contact through physical violence, sexuality, or some combination of the two.*

"When a child is chronically abused by adults who get their relational needs met in sexually perverse or aggressive ways, he or she can readily come to believe that the only way to have a relationship is through violence, sexuality, or some combination of the two."

What has been modeled for children, children tend to replicate. While children may yearn for a relationship of love, tenderness, and caring, if they have only experienced pseudo-intimacy through perverse object contact, they will tend to live out that script. Sometimes the sexually abused child believes that it is not just her aggressive and eroticized impulses that cause rejection and hurt others, but also that "one's affiliative desires are ultimately perverse, destructive of relationship, and the cause of one's own abuse. This cruel paradox, that the desire to love and be loved causes violence and perversion is, I believe, one reason that sexual abuse is so damaging to the child's sense of self and other. The child comes to believe that love destroys."

What an abyss divides such an abused person and genuine love; what a gap exists between such an abused person and the genuine love and grace of God. What sadness that some children come to believe that their love somehow causes hate.

The abused child holds on to the abusive and painful introjects "because of the fear of psychic annihilation." Being connected to the bad objects is at least better than psychological dissolution, the terrifying isolation of total disconnection (since no good objects have been deeply internalized), and being emotionally orphaned. The obstinate attachment to the bad objects functioning as ultimate authority keeps these persons from experiencing the foundational truth of life that they are the beloved children of the true Source of their life and being. As one client said to me in relation to his parental introjects, "I have it from the Highest Authority [parents] that I have no authority."

Healing and recovery are extremely difficult for such traumatized children, who have internalized "the neglectful, sexual or violent relationships to which they have been exposed. . . . The introjects of traumatized children are, in this view, simply different and 'worse' than those of children who have not suffered such violations. These introjects are harder to metabolize, not because of innate aggression or failures of integrative capacity but because the introjects encode horrific experience, impossible conflicts, and extreme defenses. The child cannot live, for example, thinking that he is completely vulnerable, but he cannot live thinking that he is utterly bad and the cause of his own violation. These dilemmas, and the anxiety they entail, literally tear the psyche apart and expose the child to the threat of psychic annihilation" (122–23).

The healing process requires the transformation of such negative introjects and that they be dethroned as the ultimate authority. The therapist or spiritual guide tries to help the person find another reality, an alternative story, that affirms in love the very being of the child and offers hope that genuine grace and love are the nature of the Eternal. In the alternative story, the cosmic projection of the ultimate power of the abusive authorities is changed, so that their lies and violent actions are no longer perceived as absolute truth. The abusers are demythologized and the abused person is detached from the abusive objects so that the person may receive the truly salvific love of God in Christ.

The Persistent Power of Erroneous Beliefs

Scripts, repetitive patterns, and the persistence of erroneous beliefs underlie many emotional and spiritual human struggles. The irrational sentences that you and I tell ourselves about our world, ourselves, and our patterns of relationship persistently sabotage our lives. Joseph Weiss, training analyst from San Francisco, has developed some ideas in this regard that may be particularly helpful to those who are rewriting a childhood script.[2] He suggests that the problems stem from "frightening unconscious maladaptive beliefs that block your functioning constructively and prevent your 'pursuit of highly adaptive and desirable goals.' " While Weiss does not speak of idolatry, his key ideas can be readily translated into that context.

1. Erroneous or pathogenic beliefs are powerful because "they are acquired in infancy and early childhood from parents and siblings, whom the child endows with *absolute authority*" (my emphasis). A child may develop pathogenic beliefs in any number of ways, such as "from trauma, instruction from and modeling by parents, from accidental events, by innocent and erroneous assumptions, etc. These beliefs about reality and morality are '*endowed with awesome authority*'" (my emphasis). Weiss infers that such idolatrous beliefs—we might also call them secular scriptures—lie at the heart of pathology.

2. Weiss also posits that there is something inherent in a person (although he does not refer to it as "the true self" or as "the image of God" in the person, as others might) that is highly motivated to disprove those beliefs. In that process, an individual with pathogenic beliefs unconsciously tests those beliefs with others, such as clergy, therapist, spiritual director, in the hope of proving those beliefs wrong. That testing may be done in words, experimental actions, or nonverbal behavior. The pathogenic beliefs have blocked the inherent, natural, spontaneous, and, theologically, the God-given goals that authorities have taught are dangerous (such as trusting one's own feelings). For instance, something happens to a child that would naturally cause her to cry, but her mother shouts at her when she cries and says, "Shut up. Go to your room. Don't be a crybaby." One such mother's favorite biblical passage was the Beatitudes, which include Jesus' words about grief: "Blessed are they that

mourn: for they shall be comforted."[3] Her little girl followed the admonition of her critical and scolding mother, instead of the truth of Jesus, as her authority.

Weiss comes close to suggesting that there are natural givens in human personality about how people are created to be loved and mirrored, and the pathogenic beliefs are oppressively laid over these normal aspects of personality. He asserts that there is an innate push or motivation to disconfirm the pathogenic beliefs and to find safe and loving relationships in which to test and live out the healthy dimensions of personality.

His ideas remind me of the story of the gentleman who went into a bargain basement clothing store to buy a suit. He tried one on that he liked in terms of style and color. He spoke to a clerk and said, "I like this suit, but the sleeves on the jacket are too long." The clerk responded, "Just hunch over your shoulders a bit and that will pull the sleeves up to the right length." The customer added, "The legs of the trousers are too long." The clerk answered, "Just bend your knees as you walk, and that will bring the trouser legs up to the correct length." The gentleman asked and received permission to wear his new suit home. As he walked out of the store with his crouched shoulders and his bent knees, two women who were entering the store noticed him. One said to the other, "Look at that poor deformed gentleman," and the other replied, "Yes, but doesn't he have a nice-looking suit on." Too often, authority figures force children into ill-fitting emotional and spiritual suits to the detriment of the authentic and true nature of the child.

3. Pathogenic beliefs act as "obstructions" when pursuing innate goals is associated with negative consequences. Weiss gives a couple of examples:

> A person "holds herself back from doing well in school because she feels her sister would be humiliated by her successes."[4]

> A person "acts aloof and distant toward her peers
> because she believes her mother will feel aban-
> doned if she has friends."[5]

Oftentimes, survivor's guilt or survivor's anxiety is attached to the obstructions. While Weiss does not use the terms "fantasy bond" or "stubborn attachment" for the negative introjects, as some do, he does believe that people are often blocked or obstructed in working toward their own goals because they fear doing so will harm someone in the family of origin or they fear someone's reaction. When a child perceives that it is unsafe to be his natural and spontaneous self, he unconsciously decides to adapt and destroy parts of his personality in order to survive in that oppressive system.

Weiss's concept of "passive-into-active-testing"[6] refers to how a person reenacts the hurtful or traumatic patterns from which he suffered by testing out those patterns on a pastor, spiritual director, or counselor by behaving "in the traumatic ways that a parent behaved toward him. The patient hopes to demonstrate that the therapist will not be upset by him as he was by his parents. He does not want the therapist to be constrained by pathogenic beliefs such as those from which he himself suffers." If such patients see that the therapist is not upset, they may be relieved. As they see the therapist dealing effectively with behavior that was traumatic for them, they may learn how to deal effectively with such behavior.[7] In theological terms, they are testing whether there is life and love beyond attacking, abusing, and crucifying the other.

Weiss's ideas can be summarized in clinical theological language. Pathogenic beliefs are secular scriptures that emanate from the false absolute authorities who are perceived as household gods by children. People long for freedom, liberation, and salvation from the tyranny of the idols, and they test others to disconfirm their irrational beliefs and idolatrous perceptions.

Exorcising Oppressive Inner Voices

Robert Firestone, a California psychologist, has developed some different as well as some similar constructs to help release people from bondage to negative parental introjects, from irrational and oppressive belief systems, and from attacking, hostile, and condemning thoughts, or "voices." In his research and clinical work, he does not speak theologically, yet he uses secular descriptions that match the ideas of clinical theology, especially of double idolatry and the tenacious covenant one has with the idol, or object of fixation. He defines "voice" as "a well-integrated pattern of negative thoughts that is the basis of an individual's maladaptive behavior."[8]

Firestone and many narrative therapists believe that "the voice is not a natural or innate part of one's personality, but that the voice [like one's personal oppressive story] is learned or imposed from without."[9] He affirms that destructive parental introjects lie behind self-attacking inner voices. The core of a person's identity is often determined by these hostile statements. While such angry voice attacks are usually more unconscious than conscious, the healing begins when, as in narrative therapy, the person identifies the self-attacks as "external attacks on the self."[10]

In the foreword to one of Firestone's books, Pamela Cantor says, "Voice Therapy is the process by which people can expose and come face-to-face with the *demons* [my emphasis] they carry."[11] In the foreword to the book *Voice Therapy,* Joseph Richman writes, "This book teaches us that these inner voices can be *exorcized* [my emphasis], and tells us how to modify or eliminate them, so as to permit adequate self-esteem and self-actualization."[12] Facing demons and exorcizing them are at the heart of voice therapy, and that makes it relevant for reauthoring and healing the spiritual life, which is often held in bondage to false gods.

Firestone uses the term "fantasy bond" to refer to the bondage by which the internalized object holds the person trapped in a persecuting emotional place, and limits the person's freedom.[13] The child is afraid of separation and the threat of psychic annihilation, and so the child seeks "to maintain the imagined safety and security of the illusory connection with the internal parent."[14] Firestone believes that exposing and dissolving such destructive fantasy bonds, along with moving toward differentiation, are essential for fulfillment in life.[15]

Voice therapy also teaches that all such voice attacks on the self have implicit or explicit death threats in them. "You are bad. You are evil. You shouldn't exist. Don't be. Don't feel what you feel. I wish you hadn't been born. Don't live more successfully or fulfillingly than I do. Drop dead." These self-destructive voices encourage self-defeating behaviors and lifestyles that Firestone calls microsuicides of everyday life. Firestone would probably agree that in the pathological process of dealing with negative introjects from the family of origin, people try to crucify, kill off, or bury certain essential parts of their being that have not been deemed acceptable by those authorities in charge.

In this vein, Firestone goes so far as to say, "We conceptualize mental illness as a subclass of suicide rather than the reverse."[16] He adds, "Thus the voice plays a major role in precipitating and maintaining a wide range of maladaptive behaviors that one *mistakenly* [my emphasis] classified or defined as a disease entity or 'mental illness.'"[17]

What a challenge to spirituality and pastoral theology that the voice of a psychic idol with its erroneous, irrational, and damning beliefs lies at the root of so-called pathology. Henri Nouwen commented in one of his last books, *Life of the Beloved,* that we tend to listen to the inner negative voices as though they represented the truth about us. Instead we should listen to and to internalize the loving affirmation of the Divine Parent, who says, "You are my Beloved, on you my favor rests."[18]

In a recent work, Firestone has added the construct of separation theory to his voice therapy. This is in recognition of many people's stubborn attachment to the voice (and to the idol) and their terror of separating from the demonic one who has defined for so many years who they are. This is like the tenacious covenant to the idol, who masquerades as the very center of a person's life and existence.

Firestone has suggested three steps that can help people reauthor their emotional and spiritual life:[19]

1. Identify and then externalize the voice, particularly in the second person, to separate the voice from the real self.
2. Reflect upon, discuss, and analyze insights and reactions to the verbalized voice, so that you may understand the relationship between your voice attacks and your self-destructive behavior patterns.
3. Formulate a rational, realistic, and objective response to the voice. Thus, you answer the voice in imagination, often with much emotional catharsis and insight.

From a pastoral theology perspective, in the three steps above you confess the idolatry, repent of it, overthrow it, and in the spirit of the good news, repudiate the old realm and the old self. Truly, this process is an exorcism of the demonic introjects that have dominated the psychological and spiritual psyche.

Overcoming Psychic Idolatry

We remain fixated to the inexorable images of our infancy and hence disinclined to the necessary passages of our adulthood.   —Joseph Campbell

Wilfred Daim was a Viennese analyst who developed the concept of psychic idolatry in a psychoanalytic context, which is particularly relevant for the theologically and spiritually minded person and professional. Daim believed that Sigmund Freud was correct in his empirical research about the object of fixation as being the root of the neurotic problem, and that the fixation was in relation to some object in childhood. Daim believed that Freud did not carry his research on fixation to its logical conclusion, and he also suggested that he did not know of any Christian analyst who had pointed out "this massive interconnection between Freud's conception of the fixation and the false absolutification."[20] Daim states: "Empirical research of analytic processes confirms that Freud was right in seeing the real root of neurosis in a fixation of the human being on an object of childhood. At closer examination, we found that in every case, the object of the fixation possesses an absolute character. The object of fixation in Freud's system is what we call an idol."[21] Daim developed his thinking in a book titled *Depth Psychology and Salvation,* spelling out in detail his ideas about idolatry and depth psychology.

Daim posits a fundamental drive (similar to that which Ronald Fairbairn speaks of in terms of the libido being object-seeking) in which the human being is seeking relationship with the Absolute and communion with the Ultimate. Daim believes that the part of the human being which is made for relationship with God is fixated on some object of childhood, and the object is given the attributes of divinity, such as omnipotence, omniscience, and omnipresence. This is somewhat similar to what Anna Freud wrote: "For the small infant, parents were the most important persons in the entire world; his infantile imagination pictured them as omniscient and omnipotent."[22] Daim emphasizes that what he calls the personality center, which is reserved for the Absolute and for communion and communication with the Absolute, is what becomes fixated around a psychic idol. Daim, like others, acknowledges that the image or the internalized negative object, is different from and may be much worse than the real parent. The idol imposes upon the fixated person the experience of degradation, disintegration, constraints, torments, and psychic suffering. Daim's thought can be summarized in his own words:

> In the course of personal development, some object is posited as absolute, and the developing human being remains affixed to this object; the development thus comes to a halt in a blind alley. This arrestation of the process of growth has a constraining and limiting effect; it has a constitutive element in the disorientation of man within the cosmos of his ontic and ontological relations; it degrades him by depriving him of his freedom to be, or to become what he ought to be. This situation has a tormenting effect upon the human person, and thus casts light upon the meaning of human suffering. All these aspects, however, converge in one focal point: they inflict harm upon the life of the psyche and tend toward psychical death as their ultimate term. This consideration leads us to the borderline of the disastrous effects of psychical fixations, that is, to the region of psychical death.[23]

Along with terror and feeling trapped in the fixation around the idol, Daim believes that the human being has what he has called "the longing for salvation."[24] People want to be saved and rescued from the internalized authority of the parental image on which they are dependent and which they have endowed with divine qualities and characteristics. They become overpowered by the idol and are held captive in the totalitarian grip of the object of fixation. Daim summarizes the main aspects of the terrifying fixation.

> [T]he object of fixation is, as mentioned before, something absolute, which possesses a quasi-godlike character; it is therefore something like an idol. Furthermore, the person is tied up with this false absolute, i.e., the temporal development is brought to a standstill by an object of fixation. In close connection with that, we can

find the fact that even in a cross-section the room for development is restricted, a fact which I call the 're-stricting element' of the fixation. . . . [T]he object of fix-ation always exercises a disorienting influence, since it tries to center all impulses for development upon itself. . . . [T]he privation of liberty, or better, the restriction of freedom which is always bound up with a fixation, is felt as the basic element of the fixation.

One who experiences "the ability to live up to one's real self, to fulfill one's true mission as a human being, feels oneself de-graded, i.e., deprived of the real dignity given to one by nature."

And this is where the inferiority complex comes in, which Adler has found in every neurosis. Since the feel-ing of lagging behind one's own ideas is to be found in any neurosis, there will also be in every case a feeling of inferiority. The normal state underlying the fixated na-ture is trying to outgrow the fixation, thus conflicting with it, so that a split will result, a fact that Bleuler calls 'ambivalence' (in principle). It is a feeling of being split up, of being torn apart between a fixation and the im-pulse of freedom; and in any case, it is experienced as something hurting, tormenting, destroying. In the ex-treme case, this means death, and the demonic purpose of any fixation is finally a special kind of killing.[25]

Daim refers to the longing for salvation as coming from the personality center. It is the existential center of the human being, and it is from this middle point that the communication with the Absolute is carried on. While the fixation brings about a captivity that affects the whole person, Daim feels that it is also right to say that one is not held captive as a whole being. That is, there is always some part of the person that is yearning and struggling for freedom or liberation, or else it would be meaningless to speak of the longing or the need for salvation. Since Daim also says that the personality center is the source of creative productivity, this creativity is also limited and blocked. Daim summarizes the meaning of this personality center that seeks to be free.

> We have characterized the personality center as the center of gravity, as the "middle point," and as the creative center of the human psyche; and above all, we have designated as its most noble and most notable task its capability of communication with God, the true Absolute. We have seen, furthermore, that with the idolization of a relative good, with the absolutization of some relative entity, the personality becomes dependent on something finite. As a matter of fact, it is the finiteness of the relativity of the idol which clothed the latter with compelling and coercive authority. Coercive compulsion thus has its origin in the fact that the personality center—actually destined for an infinite end—has become deadlocked in the finite nature of the object of fixation. . . . The personality center is never totally but only partially "fixed." This means that the personality center remains always capable of rising in a larger or smaller degree above its fixations and of partially fulfilling its naturally given tasks.[26]

Daim also focuses on the object of the longing and the desire for salvation. This essentially is the teleological dimension in which the person desires an openness toward reality, a restoration of human dignity, a freedom from the bondage to the totalitarian demands of the idol, and a sense of what Daim calls "overtness-toward-infinity." This represents the tendency of the heart or the personality center to aim for communication and relationship with a true Absolute. Daim summarizes this construct in the following way: "[T]he heart craves for a state of being open and free to God, for the right orientation, the rehabilitation of lost dignity, and finally the healing and—as far as death is concerned—for resurrection."[27]

Daim suggests that people often try to find a regressive solution to their predicament by attempting to recover the prefixation or uterine state of existence, but that this is different from the redemptive state or the state of being free from the idol. In fact, Daim also suggests that sometimes in order to avoid the agonizing struggle with the object of fixation, the idol, a person will try to escape or regress into this antecedent state of paradise. We readily think of addictions that seek to anesthetize pain and place people in their own psychic nirvana as a pseudo attempt to return to their prefixation state.

Since the object of fixation is seen as an absolute, people must believe that there is someone more powerful than the object of fixation in order to be free of the idol's totalitarian power. They sense that they do not have the innate strength to accomplish this alone, and so they look for what Daim calls a "savior." This is somewhat reminiscent of the Alcoholics Anonymous use of the concept of a "higher power" to help free people from their addiction. Those who feel that there is no power from beyond that can free them from bondage and captivity in relationship to the idol often despair. Daim says that the longing for a savior figure includes the knowledge that nothing within the person can force this power or this savior to act to free one. Daim spells this out:

> The "savior" must be a liberator: he must destroy terror, compulsion, oppression and subjugation so that the natural exigencies of human freedom can be restored. . . . It is one of the functions of the "savior" to bring about a deliverance from the idol. This means that the "savior" must first "relativitize" the idol (cut it down to size, as it were) and then utterly destroy it. . . . The "savior," furthermore, must restore the person's lost human dignity and deliver one from the degradation brought on by fixation. The savior must aid the individual in overcoming the stage of infantility and in the attainment of maturity. He must also

be capable of saving the person from painful torment. To accomplish this, the system of fixation must first be demolished. Last but by no means least, the saving power must truly be a savior in the capacity of healing wounds and regenerating nature, so that a "hale" and reintegrated human structure can arise from the former disintegration. This already implies a reawakening, a rebirth, of the soul from the state of psychical death. The "savior" must be able to impart the power which makes possible the resurrection of the soul and thus—the fulfillment of the savior's essential function—the salvation from death. . . . And if it is true that the person must be saved from a "god," it is even more certain that the one who saves must himself be of divine nature: the savior must be God. If the task to be accomplished is salvation from an idol, then— unless a new terror is to replace the old one—the Savior must be a true and real God. It is thus the true God who saves the human being from a false god.[28]

Daim is keenly aware that this salvation from the idols is not total salvation. He suggests that in this process, "the respective objects of fixation are uprooted by a revolt of the underlying healthy nature and the road is clear for a free, natural development of the human being toward God. . . . This is a process of deliverance from the fixations to idols and consequently from the blockings of the weakened will and the dimmed mind."[29]

In the process of healing, the object of fixation becomes clearer, and the need for liberation and salvation from the bad objects grows stronger, even becoming extreme. At this point, the person may look directly to a therapist, a spiritual guide, or a clergyperson to be the savior. According to Daim, the healer should not attempt to be the savior; in fact he or she may even withdraw a bit to allow the person to reach out for the Savior who actually has divine power to rescue the person from the tyranny of the idol. Then there comes a stage of strong, aggressive pushing against the idol, which destroys its arrogated absoluteness, and the whole illusory world that was structured around the idol also falls. The person may be very anxious at that time because he had found security in the attachment to the idol, and this letting go is frightening. This process of repudiation and renunciation of the idol may even happen within a span of a few hours, Daim believes. The person "seems to say to himself, 'I surrender it (the idol) and myself; I give up; I've had enough!' This kind of surrender is actually an abandonment of the person's false position which has now become untenable; a surrender, in other words, to reality and its true actual proportions and dimensions. . . . Another aspect of the same process of transformation is the definitive abandonment of the former resistance to reality—which was in the last analysis a resistance to God—and the opening up of the personality to God."[30]

The "old self" that was fixated on the idol has died, and the authentic self has emerged, as from a deep sleep, for which Daim uses the word "resurrection" to denote this emergence, or new life.

Inner Bonding of the Internal
Loving Parent and the Inner Child

Margaret Paul, a psychotherapist and clergywoman in California, has developed sophisticated and thoughtful constructs of understanding the inner child in relation to the inner loving adult/parent, in the spiritual context of a higher guidance or higher power. Paul posits that

> becoming a loving Inner Adult/Parent to our Inner Child is the key to a productive and joyful life, as well as to the ability to establish and sustain intimacy. It is not enough to tell the child within that we love and cherish him or her, and that he or she did not cause our parents to be abusive. Unless we become the parents to ourselves

that we always wanted, every moment of the day, our Inner Child will never believe he or she is really lovable. If the Adult in us does not treat the Child in us lovingly, then telling the Inner Child he or she is lovable is just lip service and will create no real change in our present life.[31]

She believes that often when parents do not give a child mature love in the family of origin, the child needs to be reconnected with the power of love for lasting healing. "The power of Inner Bonding is the power of love as the force that heals, love from Inner Adult to Inner Child. Others' love can support this process—love from mate to mate, from friend to friend, from therapist to client; but it is only when the Inner Adult loves the Inner Child that true healing and joy occur."[32]

The inner bonding process between the loving adult/parent and the inner child means that (1) people disidentify, detach, and differentiate from all the core shame-based beliefs from the family of origin which say that they are wrong, bad, or defective, and (2) people open their minds and hearts to learn of a higher source of love and truth, which they internalize, and by which they seek to orient their lives. Paul suggests that people have to move beyond twin fears learned from negative childhood authorities: first, the fear of engulfment or enmeshment, and second, the fear of abandonment and rejection. She notes that children tend to parent themselves as they were parented, an idea that is similar to the concepts of fixation, idolatry, repetition of scripts, and the ritual of destructive litanies.

Paul says that codependence exists when the inner adult abdicates responsibility for the inner child. "Codependent behavior falls into two distinct categories: (1) narcissistic or 'taking,' and (2) empathetic 'caretaking.' We operate from the overtly controlling side of codependence when we come from the belief: 'You are responsible for my feelings.' We operate from the covertly controlling caretaking side of codependence when we come from the belief: 'I am responsible for your feelings.' "[33] Paul asserts that both compulsive *takers* and *caretakers* are addicted, and both feel empty and lonely.

Paul encourages clients to conceive and experience the Core of Reality as love, and to know that they are more profoundly connected with that Loving Source of life than to their hurtful families of origin. She encourages dialogues between clients and their "Higher Power" or "Higher Loving Guidance" about their erroneous beliefs based on the false absolutes of childhood, about the nature of loving behavior toward the inner child, about the freedom to experience the totality of their feelings and needs, and about taking responsibility for their lives by choosing to be open to learning and rewriting their life stories. Thus, she challenges them to parent the inner child with the spirit of love and grace of the Divine Parent so that there is an inner bonding process of the Divine and the human.

Please reflect on these two questions that may help operationalize the above ideas: Can I pray for the courage to give up my attachment to inner authorities that do not deeply love me for myself? Can I instead listen to and internalize the love of God for my inner child?

Confessing the Meaningfulness of Our Symptoms

We should never want to take from a soul what still nourishes it, and what God allows it to sustain its weakness. To want to anticipate grace is to destroy it. —François de Fenelon

When people reach out to a counselor or spiritual director for help, they usually have a covert psychological attachment to keeping things just as they are, without being aware of their resistance to change. Most people do not know why they want to stay exactly as they are, and they are not aware that maintaining their symptoms is not as costly emotionally as giving up those symptoms would be. In other words, procrastinators may hate their inability to accomplish things on time, but they don't change because they believe, unconsciously, that being prompt would bring worse consequences than the procrastination, such as giving up their anger and attachment to authority that demands obedience. A new approach by Bruce Ecker and Laurel Hulley suggests that problems and symptoms have a coherent meaning that is beyond the person's awareness. The symptom is an important part of a person's unconscious meaning system. "The unconsciousness of the symptom's emotional truth means that symptoms are generated by living as though their emotional truth isn't the case."[34] The operative theological significance of this idea is that we tend to make psychospiritual attachments to our worldviews and self-concepts, and they are highly resistant to change. Ecker and Hulley note in their book about depth oriented brief therapy (DOBT) that "what mattered most in triggering lasting change was for the client to find in experience the already-existing but hidden emotional meaning that the problem had for him or her . . . to arrive at this point required reaching into the client's constructions operating outside of awareness. When we began intentionally to seek the problem's *emotional truth*—an unconscious construction of passionately felt meaning—from the very start of therapy, our work began to reliably achieve the level of effectiveness we were seeking."[35]

DOBT operates with two convictions: (1) "that the unconscious constructs generating the client's problem are immediately accessible and changeable from the start of therapy," and (2) "the occurrence of the presenting symptom is dictated coherently by the individual's currently operating constructions of meaning." This postmodern perspective is congenial to constructivist therapists who believe that "problems are generated entirely by the individual's cognitions and emotions comprising his or her present construction of reality."

In the constructivist view, your symptoms are the cost or consequences of your current way of construing reality. Because you are the one who set up that construction of reality in the first place, it is you who can change it, if skillfully guided to do so, in order to eliminate those consequences. Therefore, from this point of view, you have an opportunity to create new meaning and to expand your construction of reality. The therapist or spiritual director tries to help you experience what DOBT calls "the emotional truth of the symptom"—a kind of lost continent of meaning in your evolving world. Your discovery of this meaning has a liberating effect. Ecker and Hulley note that two positions are taken in relationship to symptoms, and that each person takes each of these two divergent positions or stances in regard to his or her symptoms. The Anti-Symptom Position means that you see your symptom or problem as senseless, irrational, completely valueless, and undesirable, and therefore you want to stop it. If you see yourself as the victim of the problem, then you take the symptom to mean negative things about yourself, such as being bad, defective, or stupid. In the Pro-Symptom Position, you see the symptom or problem as having deep sense and compelling personal meaning, and being vitally necessary, of such positive value that it must not simply stop. You have created and implemented the symptom you needed. The Pro-Symptom Position is unconscious, since you are unaware of how needed and meaningful the symptom really is, so a therapist, pastor, or spiritual director may believe that the symptom is meaningful and necessary to you and that unconsciously, you need it to be exactly the way it is. Through a process of "radical inquiry" or "radical discovery," you seek to find the symptom's emotional truth, which "is completely the client's own already-existing but unrecognized construction of meaning, and it is through the recognition and further evolution of that construction that change occurs in depth-oriented brief therapy." You work to discover experientially that "the emotional worth or meaningfulness of having the symptom in fact outweighs its costs." While Ecker does not directly comment on the obstinate attachment to the object of fixation, or the idol, he does note, particularly in some of his cases, that people maintain their symptoms in order to hold on to the covert attachment to the introject and/or the relationship with a person from one's family of origin. This helps to explain Ecker's major orientation to experiencing the emotional truth that lies behind resistance, which he defines "as an expression of the coherence of the client's constructions of reality." He is in agreement with systems theorist Paul Dell, who has noted that "the individual's . . . coherence is the lock and the therapist's interventions are the keys. . . . It is always the lock that determines which keys will work." Ecker and Hulley explain this interesting image of the lock and key in relation to resistance by saying,

> A wrong key indeed encounters resistance, but for the reason that it is a wrong key, not because the lock is "resisting." The lock simply has the structure it has and coherently behaves according to that structure. In precisely the same way, the therapist's experience of encountering resistance means one thing and one thing only: what the therapist is trying to do does not fit with the structure of the client's construction of reality. Therefore, the therapist should change keys rather than blame the lock. That is, rather than view the client as noncooperative, pathologically opposing health, or not yet ready for treatment, "it would be more accurate (and more honest)," according to Dell, "to say that the treatment is not yet ready for the patient."

One goal in this instance would be to help the client to name in a single statement the two sides of her struggle: "I implement the symptom of ____ for the special purpose of _____, and for me, achieving this purpose is worth specific pain and troubles that accompany the symptom." The DOBT therapist uses various techniques, including giving the client an index card at the end of the hour, on which the therapist has written as succinctly as possible the emotional truth highlighting the emotional costs of the two symptom positions. The client is asked to review the card a couple of times a day, write down any newly discovered pro-symptom positions that are operating in the person's life, and bring that record back to the next session with the therapist. For example, to a person whose identity is tied to being a loser, I might give a card that said, "As awful as it is to be a loser and a failure, it is emotionally less costly than being successful, which would threaten and upstage my wimp of a father and upset my mother, who cannot stand being in relationship with secure and successful men."

While there are many distinctive and detailed areas and points of view in the implementation of DOBT, the most important thing for our thinking here is the confessional approach to change that Ecker and Hulley take in their work. They believe that "change is blocked when the client tries to move from a position that he or she doesn't actually have as a governing emotional truth. Therefore, for the client to be free to move to a new position that is free of the symptom, first have the client take the emotionally governing, pro-symptom position he or she actually has." Here again, we find that, in regard to reauthoring one's life, the confession of the emotional and spiritual truth of what is going on with the person is primary and fundamental for change to take place. A spiritual guide or therapist who sought to impose her or his truth or story upon the client or the pilgrim would tend to block further growth and development. This nonpathological approach to dealing with human problems really offers a detailed and technical way of helping people to come to a profound confession of the emotional and spiritual truth of why they are being and functioning exactly as they are. By coming to your emotional and spiritual truth, you open up an inner freedom whereby you may have the possibility of considering other alternatives, other choices, and the expansion of your life and work.

While many theorists and clinicians would suggest that low

self-esteem is a serious problem for numerous people, Ecker suggests that low self-esteem is basically a protective action that tries to make sense of mistreatment, abuse, rejection, or neglect in your family of origin. Thus, by maintaining a sense of low self-worth, you preserve your deep intrapsychic connection with the authority figures in your family of origin. You can then avoid identifying and expressing the grief, helplessness, and anger over your parent's betrayal of you as a child and the wasted opportunities in your life. You can also protect yourself from further blows and attacks from others by low self-esteem; you can seek revenge on the family by failing; you can use low self-esteem to seek nurturance from others, avoid the frightening loss of the familiar, avoid moral accountability, and in a sense remain in or return to childhood by preserving the same role with parents at any cost. So it may be better to maintain your survival by a low self-esteem than to get over it and face worse issues. Again, this situation illustrates how you set up the authority images to function as the ultimate, and maintain a tenacious connection with the idol even though it means having low self-esteem and self-destructive attitudes. It is better to remain connected with the internalized parental image with all of its disadvantages than to lose the relationship with the idol and be out in the wilderness on your own as an orphaned wanderer.

Reflect on the following question to connect the above material with your personal experience: Do you have a problem or symptom that you perpetuate so you will not have to face something that is more threatening or upsetting to you?

A Solution-Oriented Focus

How often have you critically told yourself that you must stop some undesirable behavior, such as procrastination or drinking too much, or scolded yourself for not doing something that you felt would be good for you, such as praying regularly or keeping a personal journal? Yet you feel caught in the same old problem, and you are unable to implement a new solution. You condemn yourself as a way of trying to change, but the turnaround never takes place, or it never lasts.

What if you focused on the solution rather than on the problem? To use this perspective to reauthor your spiritual life, you will need to become aware of how the perceived problem actually began as a childhood solution to the interpersonal difficulties in your family of origin. Your emotional survival in the family depended on your developing solutions that were essential for coping emotionally in that environment. In many cases, the survival solutions were self-crucifying, self-sabotaging, and self-atoning strategies designed for survival in a world that was governed by frightening, abusive, neglectful, rejecting, or abandoning authorities. While your child self has brilliantly conceived of ways to survive, such as repression, denial, passivity, and self-loathing, by not offending the authorities, your childhood solution ultimately becomes your adult problem, such as depression and low self-esteem. You might find it helpful to recast your negative judgment about your present adult problem. Try thinking of it as an absolute necessity for your survival as a child. That may help you to be kinder to yourself so that you can stop being so harsh about what was truly a solution in your youth.

This approach asks that you focus your attention away from negativity toward yourself and the perceived failure, badness, and stuckness of your predicament. Instead, focus on those moments and places in your life in which you have succeeded and found some other solution than the old, habitual ones. Your focus is to be on those times and on those situations when you have solved the problem in a different way. For example, if you talk with a spiritual director or a counselor, you may need to discuss not just those times when the problem occurs and you feel trapped and miserable, but also reflect on exceptional, constructive solutions that you have utilized but overlooked. This approach suggests that you focus on the many hours in a week when you were not functioning by using the old solutions, but instead were operating with some different coping skills. (In dealing with people who have a drinking problem and suffer from a lapse, for example, this approach zeroes in on what enabled them to move out of and beyond the lapse rather than focusing solely on what was to blame for the lapse.)

The three rules of a solution-focused orientation are:

1. If it ain't broke, *don't fix it!*
2. Once you know what works, *do more of it!*
3. If it doesn't work, then don't do it again. *Do something different!*[36]

Some counselors use the "miracle question" approach, asking the client to imagine what the future might be like if there were a miraculous solution and the problem was finally gone. For instance, "Suppose that one night, while you were asleep, there is a miracle and the problem that brought you into therapy is solved. However, because you are asleep, you don't know that the miracle has already happened. When you wake up in the morning, what will be different that will tell you that this miracle has taken place? What else?"[37]

In a similar vein, you might ask yourself the question: if a miracle happened overnight, solving your problem, how would your spiritual story and life be different and transformed? Sometimes, being able to visualize and internally imagine the transformation enables the miracle to take place.

If you have been overly critical of yourself about difficulties of bringing about the changes in yourself that you have desired, you may be helped by the solution-oriented focus, which seeks to shift you away from the blaming and shaming of being caught in the web of childhood survival strategies. Words such as "resistant," "difficult," "defensive," "codependent," and "in denial," which tend to impute blame and guilt for one's struggles with changing, are not used in this frame of thinking.

Reflect on the fact that, while it was imperative for you to provide the self-atoning behavior in your family of origin, there is a divine solution through God's own loving and forgiving atonement in Christ. You may be able to trust in the love that is offered to you in Christ and the ultimate solution in the cross and the resurrection rather than in continuing your role as the atoning one and savior.

A Narrative Approach

Daniel Taylor writes, "You are your stories. You are the product of all the stories you have heard and lived—and of many that you have never heard. They have shaped how you see yourself, the world, and your place in it. Your first storytellers were home, school, popular culture, and perhaps, church. Knowing and embracing healthy stories are crucial to living rightly and well. If your present life story is broken or diseased, it can be made well. Or, if necessary, it can be replaced by a story that has a plot worth living."[38]

Narrative therapy, as developed by Michael White of Australia and David Epston of New Zealand, is a hopeful approach to change because it holds the belief that all people have the inherent power to liberate themselves from the oppressive and depressing stories of their personal history. In this process, a clinician, a pastor, a spiritual guide, or a friend may help you realize that the story by which you have lived your life is not a story of truth and reality. Rather, it is a story, as White and Epston suggest, that is psychologically and politically oppressive, dominating, and unjust. From a pastoral perspective, the story is a lie masquerading as gospel truth, and it is written for you by your internalized object that functions deceitfully as ultimate truth and reality. So the goal in many ways is to recognize from the narrative perspective that you are never the problem. "Neither the person nor the relationship between persons is the problem. Rather, the problem becomes the problem, and then the person's relationship with the problem becomes the problem."[39] In other words, the narrative approach seeks to liberate you from your faulty self-identity and to externalize the problem and the story as being separate from your own true self. You are encouraged to consider yourself as one who can reauthor the oppressive and undermining aspects of your previous, dominant story. White and Epston explain the process of externalization as follows: "Externalizing is an approach to therapy that encourages persons to objectify and, at times, to personify the problems they experience as oppressive. In this process, the problem becomes a separate entity and thus external to the person or relationship that was described as the problem. Those problems that are considered to be inherent, as well as those relatively fixed qualities that are attributed to persons and to relationships, are rendered less fixed and less restricting." [40]

Narrative therapists, like solution-oriented therapists, ask their clients to review their life history and to focus on those times when the oppressive story did not have control over their lives. People are advised to look for the exceptions or the unique outcomes in their life history which may provide the means by which they can begin to rewrite the narrative of their life. Those exceptions are like those sparkling moments when the person has not been dominated by the problem. An example of this approach would be a person who was generally reserved, self-conscious, and frightened in new social situations, but who, on one or two particular occasions, was able to enter the social arena with assertiveness and confidence. The narrative therapist would try to build on that kind of constructive exception and positive moment.

John Byng-Hall, in *Rewriting Family Scripts,*[41] notes that people function by using one of three scripts: "replicative scripts" involve scenarios that have been passed on as guiding myths, stories, and beliefs from generation to generation. Those who use "corrective scripts" have chosen an opposite style of functioning because of pain, disappointment, and discomfort with the stories and scripts that were imposed on them in childhood. "Improvised scripts" are myths, stories, and styles that are either spontaneously improvised or influenced by learning from other people as the life story is rewritten.

The narrative approach assumes that there is an underlying constructive and creative self that has been overlaid and oppressed by stories that have led the person to develop a false identity. Narrative therapists speak of the story "living the client," and thus the story needs deconstructing and revising into a proactive and reauthored new story. It is really a process of demythologizing the old story and remythologizing a new story. Parry and Doan note: "The importance of the revision phase of the therapy cannot be overemphasized. It is one thing to be a catalyst in the deconstruction of clients' or families' mythology; it is another to provide them with the opportunity to revise their stories in such a way that these will be more in line with what they want. To omit the revision process is to leave the clients in a state of 'psychological free-fall.' Alternatively stated, it is to leave them outside of a story."[42]

A theological critique of the narrative approach shows that there is a certain relativity and subjectivity to the creation of the stories. From a Christian vantage point, reauthoring or rewriting can be more accurately done in relation to the revealed story of the good news of God in Jesus Christ. In other words, your view of ultimate reality, of your neighbor, and of yourself are more clearly understood in the context of the Christian revelation than simply from your own perspective. This approach, however, must not impose the gospel on people's lives and their reauthored stories, but rather it suggests that the reauthoring process take into account the biblical revelation so that the reauthored story is grounded in the ultimate reality of the good news.

To its credit, narrative therapy does take oppressive systems and forces into consideration, such as racism and sexism, which can play such a destructive part in people's lives. In the reauthoring process, narrative therapy seeks to help people include cultural systems of social injustice in externalized problems and stories, and to help them find the unique outcomes that are necessary for resisting oppressive forces. This is one of the reasons that some have said that narrative therapy has a kinship with liberation theology in its desire to free people from oppressive systems.

One technique used in narrative therapy that can be helpful in rewriting your spiritual life is to give one title to the old oppressive story and another to the revised or reauthored story. For example, one person titled his old story "The Failure and the Loser." The title he gave to his revised story was "The Resilient Come-Backer."

The transformations you experience as you rewrite your story can be made more permanent and concrete if you have the support of individuals and organizations in your own social sphere. In working consistently toward such a positive social reinforcement, narrative therapy challenges the church to think about its place in being able to mirror and affirm the growth and development in the lives of its members as well. Church people who have lived under condemnation from childhood need to experience the church incarnating love and grace in its ministry and stories.

Narrative therapy is reminiscent of Jesus' words when he said, "It was said by them of old . . . but I say unto you that . . . "[43] In other words, there is a demythologizing of that which was seen as authoritative in the past or as the previous central plot to your life so that now the religious community and the gospel may provide a counterplot and new creative authority of God in Christ.

There is a postmodern constructivist psychological perspective and a New Age spiritual point of view that hold that content is irrelevant, that there is no revealed truth, but only constructed stories, and that going with the flow or with the experience itself is what really counts. I suggest that as you reauthor the story of your spiritual life, it is critically important that you consider "not just the experience itself, but also the content of the experience. A real authority . . . is indeed within experience, but it is not the authority of experience, it is an authority for experience, it is an authority experienced."[44] That means that your soul must take its stand on something more than your subjective impressions so that it is not the experience itself that has sole authority, but rather authority also involves the nature of the gospel of love and grace. Too often, people in their attempt to get free from authoritarian dogma, institutions, and religion, throw out the baby with the bath water and simply go back to human experience as the only source of authority, since they see the other, more traditional authorities as oppressive, unjust, and destructive. However, as the revealed truth of the Christian faith affirms, there is a Story beyond a story, a God beyond the gods, and an Ultimate Reality beyond all perceptions of reality. Thus, for the fullest experience of psychological and spiritual well-being, you need to rewrite your story in relation to the ultimate truth of the revealed faith.

REWRITING YOUR WORK, LEADERSHIP, AND CAREGIVING PATTERNS

▲▲▲▲▲▲▲▲▲

*T*he basic relationship patterns developed for
adapting to the parental family in childhood are
used in all other relationships throughout life. The
basic patterns in social and work relationships are
identical to relationship patterns in the family.
                                              —Murray Bowen

*W*hen it comes time to do your own life, you
either perpetuate your childhood or you stand on
it and finally kick it out from under.
                                              —Rosellen Brown

In the early 1970s, I attended a conference in western Massachusetts called "The Use of the Self in Family Therapy." A parade of family therapy pioneers, such as Virginia Satir, spoke to the professional audience without any speaker knowing what the previous presenters had said. The most fascinating and memorable fact of that conference was that each speaker early in the lecture mentioned in so many words that "I was trained to be a family therapist by the age of five in my family of origin." All of us, regardless of our roles and jobs, have learned our patterns of coping, our dynamics of reacting, and even our vocational roles from our family of origin.

Rabbi Edwin H. Friedman has been a leader in pointing out that the key to leadership, whether in churches, businesses, government service, or clinical work, is the individual's capacity for differentiation from the family of origin. He believes that the most vital factor in changing any system or family is the capacity of the "leader to define his or her own goals and values while trying to maintain a nonanxious presence within the system."[1] "Self-definition is a more important agent of change than expertise," he says, and "both congregational and personal families tend to reverse the priorities of expertise and self-definition, particularly when they become anxious."[2] This definition of leadership contains echoes of Jesus' words about differentiating from (hating) one's family of origin in order to be his disciple.

This approach has been carried forward into other work systems beyond the church and synagogue. Family ghosts can appear in any workplace, and patterns from people's families of origin are replayed in the marketplace and office as well as in religious institutions.

A child is often given an irrational role assignment or designated place in the family of origin, and this internalized family baggage is carried over unconsciously into the workplace and into the church. David Ulrich and Harry Dunne note that there are family mandates that are "laid down by past generations of family members concerning what new members of this family are to be, to do, and to stand for. While children may accept their designated place out of fear of being left with no place at all, the principal holding power of designation comes from the child's loyalty, his or her sense of what is owed in exchange for having received life and nurture." They also observe that, while to some people "the notion of adults being bound by designations laid down for them in their childhood—the notion that grandma may have something to do with how you respond to your boss—may seem absurd, it is by now well recognized that when an employee enters the workplace, the family baggage does not get checked at the door. The old patterns of attitude and action are ready to be called up, and it is remarkable how easily one can find actors at work who are ready and willing to stand in for the missing family members. The workplace is actively conducive to the playing out of designations."[3]

While it behooves all of us to review how our work relationships may be re-creations of our patterns of relating learned in our family of origin, it is especially important for church leaders, both lay and professional, to assess their helping roles in their respective ministries to others. While the following material may apply more to those in ministry, especially in pastoral counseling, it is also relevant for our care giving roles with friends and relatives.

Many caregivers are unconsciously caught up in trying to heal members of their family of origin, who are projected unconsciously onto those they seek to help. Often such caregivers have an intense need to transform and heal others in order to feel that they themselves are in a good place. They may be avoiding the hard work of experiencing their sadness and powerlessness in their inability to change and heal their parents and others in their family of origin. It is no wonder that these spiritual caregivers get angry and frustrated with those who resist their help, because these helpers believe that their own place in the world depends on getting others to change. When people realize that the caregiver has an imperative need to heal and change them, resistance is automatic because the person being helped does not feel unconditional love and acceptance. Behind these caregivers' intensity about healing others and their irritation at others who do not change is unresolved grief, sadness, helplessness, and powerlessness about growing up in a family system in which they could not alter and heal significant persons. They are

unconsciously trying to accomplish in their vocation and present relationships and systems what they could not achieve in
their childhood families. When they were young, their safety, security, and well-being seemed to depend on getting others in the
family to function differently, but adult caregivers cannot be
truly helpful if their own sense of well-being is dependent on
change and growth in others.

Every time you as a spiritual leader give away your power to
someone you are trying to help—meaning that the person must
get better for you to feel all right, successful, or effective—then
there will be an impasse in the helping relationship. It is only in
the full experience of your own sadness and powerlessness to
change and to heal the significant figures of your childhood that
you as a helper are free not to implicitly demand that others "get
well" or "get their act together." This perspective is like that of
the parishioner with a serious drinking problem whose pastor
was feeling very proud that his parishioner, whom he was counseling, was sobering up, until one day the parishioner went on a
serious drinking binge. When asked later what had happened,
the parishioner said, "I felt my pastor was like a spiritual canni-
bal who was going to hang me as another trophy on his helping
belt, and I wasn't going to let myself be used that way." Thus his
binge was to defeat the pastor and to maintain his own integrity,
even at the great price of a relapse.

The unconscious strategy of salvation for many of us as caregivers is to avoid bearing the unbearable feelings of sadness,
hurt, powerlessness, anger, helplessness, and anxiety from our
childhood families, and to try to repress and transcend those
feelings by healing and transforming others in our pseudo-
savior role as helper and caregiver. Igor Caruso, a psychologist,
has pointed out that healers and caregivers must come to terms
with the "Christ-archetype" in themselves. Of the analyst, Caruso
writes: "If the analyst has no support in the conscious cleansing
of the 'Christ-archetype,' he is in danger of becoming fascinated

with his own role as redeemer. The psychoanalyst's terrible temptation, which is not made any easier by the fact that in most cases it remains unconscious, is to become God and play Christ."[4] If we have played that healing, rescuing role in our families of origin and if we repeat that role in our ministries, work, and interpersonal relationships, we are doomed to a lot of frustration and unhappiness, and we will not experience the reality of grace and love which comes to us from our true Savior.

There is no guarantee, however, that therapy, spiritual direction, self-help literature, spiritual retreats, and the like will free you from the clutches of the tenacious idol. Unless there is the direct awareness of and the affective encounter with the false gods, no fundamental spiritual transformation takes place. You must confess and repent that an introject or introjects has functioned as the supreme authority in your psyche to have the freedom to choose to respond to the true God who chooses us in love.

Case Example

A priest named Jason had all the right credentials, but he was still controlled by the object of his childhood fixation. Jason had had years of therapy with various therapists, years of spiritual direction with different spiritual directors; he had attended many spiritual retreats with various formats; and he had a sound theological education, a doctorate in pastoral counseling, years of supervised clinical experience, and lots of professional experience. But Jason was stuck, even though he was not conscious of that. He was an overly responsible, overly committed, overly extended compulsive pastor who was an exhausted victim of people and institutions who needed and expected too much of him. He had little awareness that this central role of his priesthood, of being overwhelmed, was the role of his childhood, which attached him to both of his parental introjects. His mother was an alcoholic who was congenial on occasion, but she was basically unreliable and undependable. Therefore, like many adult children of alcoholics, Jason became a parentified child in relationship to his mother. So, he parented his mother like the old song said, "I'm my own grandpa." He saw his father as a flake and a wimp. He, too, was not trustworthy, and he was neither an advocate for his only child, Jason, nor was he willing to be a firm adult instead of an enabler with his alcoholic wife.

So it did not take the brains of a rocket scientist for Jason as a little boy to figure out that his survival in his unreliable family of origin depended on his being the rescuer, helper, and savior. What he had not come to grips with in adulthood was that he still maintained the operative worldview that there is an unreliable and undependable ultimate authority, clumsily and ineptly in charge of the universe, without any efficacious, incarnate intervention to guide, help, and save the people in need. Thus Jason still had to play a pseudo-savior in church, counseling, religious community, friendships, and so on. He was stuck with the idolatry of a perceived weak and ineffective god and a defensive survival strategy of hanging himself on a cross of overresponsibility to save the people around him and himself.

In solution-oriented therapy, we see that Jason's solution to survival in his family, which was to be the overfunctioning, parentified child and savior, became his adult problem and sin (replacing Jesus Christ as Savior), and that his overfunctioning did not gain him salvation. Jason had also been able to avoid facing his inner child's terror of being psychologically abandoned by both of his parents. His separation anxiety was too much to tolerate, and therefore he strove mightily to work so hard on everyone's behalf that they would not reject him. His overresponsibility was his self-atonement, as he could not believe in his heart that there was a loving God who would bridge the gap in initiatory love and make the divine atonement that was accomplished in Jesus Christ. While Jason's espoused or professed theology was about love and grace, his operative theology was fashioned in the cauldron of his family of origin in which he had to be the pseudo-savior in an untrustworthy world.

One could interpret Jason's exhaustion, overscheduling, and inability to set responsible limits and boundaries in his life as cries for help, for liberation from the demanding and oppressive tyranny of the idol. His covert prayer was, "O God, keep me strong, empower me, and make me superman. Keep me from any dependency, any needs and feelings of my inner child, and from the anxiety of not being in control. Amen." His secular scripture was clearly, "Unless you become as a strong parent, you will not enter the realm of God."

Jason is a prototype of many caregivers, church leaders, and religious professionals who do many fine things and contribute productively in numerous ways. However, in their heart of hearts, they are still in bondage to the psychic idols of their youth. The lens through which they see the world and the self-atoning and self-destructive patterns they use as coping strategies are constantly repeated in a wide variety of settings and relationships. While they are consciously followers of Jesus, deep inside they are still slaves of their inner pharaohs, from whom they are terrified to separate and go out into the wilderness toward freedom. Those who seek to call them forth from their tyrannical idols are sometimes condemned as enemies, even as the Hebrews got upset with Moses as he led them in the exodus. Spiritual transformation in many ways is a liberation process from the inner land dominated by the idolatrous pharaohs, who constrain us in emotional slavery and spiritual bondage.

Freedom from Emotional Reactivity

All of us have our emotional "hot buttons" that get pushed by family, friends, work associates, church members, and so on. These hot buttons and our impulsive emotional reactions are usually generated from relationships and experiences in our family of origin. The spiritual journey invites us to an ever-expanding internal freedom so that when our hot buttons are pushed, as inevitably they will be, we can proactively choose among various alternative responses. To be an effective spiritual person, you need to become aware of these repeated automatic reactions to others when your hot buttons are pushed so that you can rewrite your response to those situations in a creative and loving way.

In a doctoral project, Wayne Kendall interviewed five pastors who had served what Edwin Friedman calls "pill" churches (as compared to "plum" churches). In all instances, the "pastors were surprised to discover how often difficult churches and problematic parishioners had triggered off a restructuring of some patterns from childhood."[5] The pastors saw with new insight how the troublesome, controlling, pouting, angry, rebellious, narcissistic, sulking, critical, depressed, and judgmental people in the congregation repeatedly tapped into the pastors' unresolved feelings toward some similarly difficult figures from their childhood, usually a parent figure. For example, pastors often found that the group in the church who tended to be dominating, controlling, arrogant, and dictatorial triggered off the reactions the pastors had had to a dominant, authoritarian parent. And those members in the congregation who tended to be quiet, sit on the sidelines, and not intervene against the church dictators aroused feelings the pastors had held toward a distant or absent parent who operated like a wimp in relationship to the dominant parent. The triangle from the family of origin was replicated in the experience in the parish without the pastor's having been previously aware of the similar dynamics.

Hurtful and upsetting situations with significant people in our lives can be reframed from the vantage point that they may allow us to see that they re-create unresolved dynamics and patterns of childhood relationships from the family of origin which we need to heal in ourselves. If we have recurring dreams, often we recognize that the unconscious is knocking on our psychic door, noting that there is a problem asking for resolution. Likewise, when there is a repetitive conflict in the external world in which we have a sense of unfreedom and defensiveness, we need to think consciously about the opportunity to utilize those difficult circumstances to enable us to find new, more differentiated ways of coping in the world of difficult relationships and institutions.

Utilizing Spiritual Direction and Counseling

In the journey of reauthoring your spiritual life, it is often helpful to have guidance from a spiritual director, a pastoral counselor, or a spiritually oriented therapist. This guide can help you name the relationships, experiences, patterns, and barriers that have impeded your connection with divine love and grace. In inquiring about such a guide or counselor, it is appropriate to ask if that person uses the family of origin as a key construct in his or her psychospiritual guidance and counseling. Your guide or counselor will generally use techniques and skills that will help liberate you from the past so that you can move toward the promised land of abundant living.

Supervision of Work and Ministry in the Context of the Family of Origin

This section is mainly for those persons, generally clergy, counselors, and spiritual directors, who give and/or receive supervision as a part of their work.

Supervising lay and pastoral ministry, without reference to the families of origin of the parties involved, is like discussing theology without reference to God. While supervision deals with intellectual knowledge, technical skills, and interpersonal relationships, it is like overlooking the elephant in the living room to neglect the central role of the family of origin in receiving professional supervision of one's work and one's religious leadership. Supervision in the context of the family of origin can be framed as the encounter of the gods of the parties involved. The implicit religious drama or operative theology of these persons, derived originally from their childhood families, is a critical focus for the actual supervision.

For example, in pastoral counseling this approach acknowledges that the original worldviews and meaning systems of the client, counselor, and supervisor have been shaped in the cauldron of the family of origin. Most of the underlying problems of clients have their roots in their childhood histories; most of the impasses that counselors experience in the therapeutic process are related to unresolved countertransference issues stemming from the therapist's family of origin; and most of the frustrations and blocks in the supervisory relationship are due to repressed materials from the childhood families of the supervisor or the counselor.

Thus, supervision of spiritual leaders must recognize the key context of the family of origin in which the maps of perceived reality, the meaning and belief systems, the mental representations of God and of self, and the operative theological worldviews have been developed, and which often stand in need of transformation in all parties involved.

Conclusion

In *A Testament of Devotion,* Thomas Kelly, the Quaker mystic, speaks most convincingly of the need to ground our ministries and our work in the Eternal Now. Kelly believes that the fevered life of religiously busy people and our taking on the primary responsibility for the healing and salvation of others lead us away from Divine Love. He writes,

> The energizing, dynamic center is not in us but in the Divine Presence in which we share. Religion is not *our* concern; it is God's concern. The sooner we stop thinking *we* are the energetic operators of religion and discover that God is at work, as the Aggressor, the Invader,

the Initiator, so much the sooner do we discover that our task is to call people to *be still and know,* listen, hearken in quiet invitation to the subtle promptings of the Divine. Our task is to encourage others first to let go, to cease striving, to give over this fevered effort of the self-sufficient religionist trying to please an external deity. Count on God knocking on the doors of time. God is the Seeker, and not we alone; God is anxious to swell out our time-nows into an Eternal Now by filling them with a sense of Presence. I am persuaded that religious people do not with sufficient seriousness count on God as an active factor in the affairs of the world. . . . Too many well-intentioned people are so preoccupied with the clatter of effort to do something *for* God that they don't hear God asking that God might do something *through* them.[6]

God invites us, whether lay or professional, to participate as God's beloved children in our spiritual work of caring, implementing justice, healing, and helping. The God beyond our gods is in loving charge, and we can rejoice that we share the good news of the gospel, and we do not create it and carry it by ourselves.

Renewing Your Spirit by Reauthoring Your Childhood Story

▲▲▲▲▲▲▲▲▲

It is better to practice it (compunction of the heart) than to know how to define it.
                              —Imitation of Christ

This chapter will focus on techniques of differentiating yourself as much as possible from your family of origin, so that you become aware of false projections onto God and the transference of erroneous beliefs to God, and open your heart and mind to receiving the true nature of God, especially God's love and grace, into your depths.

The centerpiece of my thesis about reauthoring your spiritual life is that first you must become as fully aware and conscious as possible of those internalized authorities which are presently functioning as the supreme power in your life. In religious language, you need to confess what false authorities are masquerading as the true Divine in your psyche. In that process, you need to be able to imagine, visualize, externalize, and have "empty chair" conversations with those powerful introjects.

Then the second step is to become as fully conscious as possible of your defensive strategy of salvation, of your childhood solution for surviving in a world governed by false ultimate authorities, of your crucifixion of parts of your personality through such psychological processes as repression, denial, low self-esteem, depression, self-destructive behaviors, self-atoning mechanisms like overachievement or self-hatred, and so on. You must confess that you have tried to be your own pseudo-Christ or pseudo-savior. As I have occasionally said in confronting a person who was particularly proud of his or her self-sacrificing atonement strategies, "Jesus only hung on the cross for three hours, and you have been hanging on your cross for thirty-five years."

The confession of both idolatries—(1) of the perceptions of ultimate reality as governed by introjects from the family of origin, and (2) the patterns of self-crucifixion, whereby you sought to survive in a world cruelly governed by false authorities—is absolutely essential to open the inner heart to the presence of the true God and the authentic Savior.

What I am seeking to spell out are the psychological and spiritual processes that are involved in 1 John 5:21, "Little children, keep yourselves from idols—false gods" (from anything and everything that would occupy the place in your heart due to God, from any sort of substitute for God that would take first place in your life.)[1]

In addition, you should look at the exceptions in your life, the times when it appears that unconditional love and grace are on the inner throne guiding your life, so that you can build on those unique outcomes. For example, I sometimes suggest that clients reflect on those people in their extended families or beyond who communicated a sense of mirroring love and validating grace to them. Oftentimes, people get so focused on the connections with the hurtful authorities that they forget to take into account the gracious and loving dimensions of other people who have treated them with respect.

In addition to the genogram work mentioned previously, the

following techniques may be used for self-understanding, or used in spiritual direction or pastoral counseling.

Voicing Your Critic and Judge

Sometimes it helps if you take the role of your own critic and judge and become that authoritarian, condemning voice against you. As you do so, consider whether those voices have been absolutized in your psyche. For example, on one early morning as I was doing my meditation and writing in my journal about why it was difficult for me to break through certain barriers to writing this book, I spontaneously became the critical voice of my father speaking at me: "You can't do it. You will fail. You are stupid. You are incapable. You are inferior. You are inadequate. You ought not succeed. What you write will be a joke; you will be criticized, laughed at, and ridiculed. So find reasons for putting off writing and do other things first." I then concluded with the following irrational statement: "My father's attitude toward me is the ultimate truth about me. My father's definition of me is the only true source of my identity and worth. My father's assessment of me carries more weight than God's evaluation of me." And then, with tongue-in-cheek, I added, "This book is dedicated to my father, who wants to sabotage its production and to defeat the writer. Or perhaps it is the nonbook which I dedicate to him."

Many of us suffer from such a voice of nagging negativity. Our obedience to that idolatrous voice, which we may despise even as we obey it, may paralyze our creativity and stifle our productivity. In this vein, the early twentieth century English Congregationalist Peter Taylor Forsyth wrote "salvation means acquiring a new and final authority."[2] For me, it is writing the book in the context of the New Creation governed by the supreme power of love and grace versus writing it under the condemning governance of the old era of the household gods of youth.

Various active methods of direct communication can be used

to get at the emotional and spiritual truth that holds us in bondage to the family of origin. Murray Bowen, James Framo, Don Williamson, and countless others have written about ways in which a person can caringly seek to communicate with the authorities of the past. Adults are sometimes surprised when they talk with their parents in an interested, questioning way (see Williamson's *The Intimacy Paradox* for an elaborate set of questions)[3] about who the parents are and what their developmental life experience has been like. Often it is helpful to get in touch with the childhood experiences and feelings of the parents in order to understand the parents' formative years and then the development of the parents' marital relationship. This process of demythologizing the parents on the one hand and humanizing them on the other often helps an adult child understand, forgive, and reconcile with the parents. This process also may lead to what Williamson speaks of as "graduation" from being the dependent child of the parent(s) to being an adult in relation to them. Likewise, this differentiation process may help free us to be connected with the Divine Mother/Father who seeks our well-being and wholeness.

The Empty Chair, Letter Writing, and Graveside Conversation

Some find helpful the empty chair method: you place the difficult part of a parent, grandparent, or sibling's personality in a chair and then have an imaginary conversation with that person about the emotional truth that has never been communicated effectively between you. It is important to distinguish between the whole person and the difficult and problematic part of that person which we place in the chair. For instance, we want to be clear that Daddy is not totally a dragon. Sometimes you may learn a lot about the other person after confronting the negative authority image by going over and sitting in the empty chair and trying to be the tender, vulnerable core of the other person and to respond in a non-defensive manner. Connecting with the inner child of the parent and with the vulnerable aspects of the parent's personality sometimes brings understanding, forgiveness, and reconciliation.

If a parent, sibling, or other significant relative is dead, or if it is clearly unwise to open up personal communication with the person for some reason, you might try writing unmailed letters to that person and discuss them with a pastor, counselor, or spiritual director. After writing your emotional and spiritual truth to that person, sometimes it is helpful to write an imagined response from the tender, vulnerable core of the recipient. The new freedom and forgiving connections found through these procedures may open up expanded places in your heart and mind to receive more fully the true nature of God's love and grace.

Some people find that going to the cemetery and having imaginary conversations with deceased relatives can be very liberating. Several times I have gone to the cemetery where my father and my two mothers are buried together. There I was able to rant and rave, cry, be grateful, express love—to share the gamut of my feelings. I found that I needed to express to them things that I had not been able to say before, so that I could be free to move to a deeper intimacy with God. Then my communication with my Divine Mother/Father could be richer and unencumbered by my attachments to my idols.

Parenting Ourselves

It may help if you think about how you are parenting yourself. We tend to parent ourselves as we were parented. If your parents neglected you or were dependent on you, for example, you may find that you busily pay attention to the needs of others but neglect your inner child, just as you were neglected. While you may profess the love of God toward you, you may not have internalized that love as the new parenting of your inner child. So in an unconscious way, you may be rejecting the parental love of God by neglecting and mistreating your inner child. At one point in my spiritual journey, my spiritual director asked if I could give a name to my inner child. I fumbled and stumbled for months, coming up with various names, none of which really seemed to fit. Then one day while reading 1 John, I came across the passage, in 4:16, "And we know [understand, recognize, are conscious of by observation and by experience], and believe [adhere to and put faith in and rely on] the love God *cherishes* for us."[4] While it was uncomfortable and awkward for me at the time, I did name my inner child: Cherished. Sometime later, my inner child felt mirrored by Henri Nouwen's book *Life of the Beloved*,[5] in which the words "beloved" and "cherished" were essentially interchangeable.

Paradox

Utilizing paradox in a variety of ways may help you bring to the surface the dynamics of your relationships with others, God, and self, and enhance your freedom to choose whether you want to continue the old patterns or select new ones. Some patterns change as you apply logic, reason, and rationality. But often the dynamics that control our lives are not logical, rational, and reasonable. Thus, it is often best to use nonrational means to address nonrational dynamics and beliefs.

In the paradoxical method we call prescribing the symptom, the procrastinating person, for example, tells himself that it is imperative *not* to get the sermon written on time, the project completed by the due date, and so on. If this procrastinating person is resistant to an internal idol dictating his or her schedule, then the integrity of that person is wrapped up in not conforming to those tyrannical demands. By putting the "shoulds" and the "musts" in the opposite direction from those dictated by the idol, and by looking at good subjective reasons for procrastinating, the procrastinator may find a freer internal space for expanding options and choices.

Another example is the person who has known "smother love"

and is highly resistant to a disciplined commitment of deepening her life of intimacy with God through prayer. She can tell herself, or a counselor or spiritual director could suggest, that it would be dangerous for her to try to get close to God through prayer and a disciplined spiritual life because she could then lose her essential identity, as happened previously with the engulfing and enmeshing parent. A spiritual guide, in this instance, does not have to function like a defense attorney for the Almighty, but rather the guide can help the pilgrim more readily by appreciating, mirroring, and empathizing through paradox with the person's profound fear of losing her personhood if she gets close to Divine Love, which she perceives as divine smother love.

This paradoxical method of joining the resistance is at its root accepting people as they are, along with their subjective good reasons, which are usually unconscious or denied. It is a process of helping people to name, claim, and confess that they really need to be the way they are for significant reasons, of which they are often unaware.

While there are innumerable ways to help yourself and others experience an alternative reading of reality in the New Creation—a reading unlike the one modeled and taught in your family of origin—let us look at some issues, questions, and suggestions that pull together key dimensions of the spiritual transformational process.

Patterns of Relationship
with Human and Divine Authority

In my own spiritual journey, I have found it helpful to reflect on how my patterns of relationship, especially with my father and two mothers, have impacted my relationship with God. I have not done this systematically, but rather as the Spirit moved me.

You may wish to write the essence of each issue on a separate piece of paper or on a separate page in your journal, and then work on one as you are moved to do so.

1. Describe and/or draw the major images or mental representations of God, both positive and negative, that have played a significant part in your life. Trace the connections between those images of God and the human relationships that helped to form those mental representations, some of which are false authorities.

2. Describe the solutions for survival that were necessary for you to live in a world so governed by those false authorities. Reflect on how those coping mechanisms for survival became elevated to the status of defensive strategies of salvation.

3. Write out a Decalogue of rules, beliefs, and injunctions from your family of origin (and other sources) that operated as commandments and secular scriptures in your inner world. Then write your Revised Decalogue of beliefs and principles that have their source in the genuine mind, heart, and spirit of God in Christ.

4. Write a title to the story that was given to you as a child, and then write a title to your reauthored story, which you have coauthored with your true Creator. Give a name to your inner child from the authorities of childhood, and then give your inner child a name from the perspective of Divine Love.

5. Identify and describe any self-atonement procedures that you used under the aegis of your family of origin, including self-destructive, underachieving, overly responsible, and overachieving patterns. Did you have any experiences in your family of origin where someone atoned on your behalf for some error of your commission or omission, and have you been able to see a glimpse of the forgiving God in Christ in their behavior?

6. Describe any images you have of Jesus Christ that are related to persons from your family of origin. For example, was there anyone in your youth who functioned as an advocate, a rescuer, a healer, an elder brother, or a savior, who provided a prototype of the cosmic advocacy, healing, and redemption by Jesus Christ? Is there any sense of disconnection from Christ as Advocate and Savior because of the lack and absence of human beings who modeled that kind and quality of caring for you?

7. Were there any times in your life when you were so central or indispensable to holding your family or some family member together emotionally, to providing comfort and counsel for family members, or for being the rational center of communication that you developed a sense of pride or messianic glory for being an indispensable comforter, consoler, mediator, and burden bearer for others? Did your family give you the irrational role assignment of being a pseudo-Christ or rescuer and savior for them? If you played this role, what have been the difficulties in abdicating this essential place of significance and value and letting God in Christ be the Comforter, Healer, and Savior?

8. What patterns of self-justification did your family of origin model in their behavior or in their expectations of your behavior? Were there ways in which you could earn approval, love, and acceptance, a pattern of justification by works and merit on the interpersonal level? Have you consciously or unconsciously transferred these patterns to a god of conditional love so that you have to earn that god's approval by your good works and meritorious behavior?

9. What anxiety or uncomfortable feelings do you need to bear so that they do not hold sway over you and

dominate you with an ultimate power? Can you name your terror and fear? For example, for me it was separation anxiety and the feared annihilation of my identity. Then, can you bear the unbearable and with the grace of God and support of others, face the terror and disempower the fear?

10. Under what circumstances, in what situations, and in what relationships, do you tend to end up in what has been called shame jail or guilt prison? Do you automatically accept the guilt and shame as true and correct? Do you raise serious questions about the authority of the guilt-inducing and shaming voices? Do you question whether those condemning voices represent the God of love and grace in Jesus Christ or whether they represent an oppressive idol or idols? Do you ask in prayer for the advocacy and courage of God in Jesus Christ to name false guilt as false guilt, to challenge the shaming beliefs as lies, and to heal your unhealthy and false guilt and shame? Do you pray for the awareness that your healthy and responsible guilt may be that you are submissive or passive to the idol and that you have not been lovingly faithful to the One who is lovingly faithful to you? Do you internalize in a meaningful way the biblical truth of "Against thee, thee only, have I sinned"?[6] Do you receive the forgiving grace of God with joy in that miraculous love for you?

11. Do you have the capacity to be nonreactive emotionally when you are criticized and judged unfairly? Do you have the capacity to respond in peace to either praise or criticism? Does your negative reaction to criticism unmask your covert pride? Are you able in a proactive way to say "So what?" in terms of letting go of your reputation and your ego when someone gossips, judges, or rejects you? Are you able to follow in

the footsteps of Jesus in terms of spiritual maturity and turn the other cheek, forgive seventy times seven, and love the enemy, the stranger, and the one who is different from you?

12. Does your selfless, giving, caring, and unselfish manner of helping and interacting with other people mask the subtle sin of pride in your unselfish love and thoughtful giving to others? Do you, as Fenelon suggests, "seek in the world also the glory of unselfishness and generosity"?[7] Do you covet the "pleasure of loving unselfishly? . . . For what is there sweeter and more flattering to a sensitive and delicate self-love than seeing itself praised as though it were not self-love?"[8]

13. Do you pray that God will give you the courage and the insight to face and to overcome any patterns, fixations, attachments, and idolatries that keep you from receiving the love and grace of God in Christ and responding lovingly with your whole being?

These questions and issues have emerged from my spiritual struggles and have helped me become aware of my inadequate mental representations of God and of Jesus Christ. They have helped me to confess my sin of worshiping false gods as well as repenting of my own usurpation of the Savior's role with its messianic glory. They have been significant as I reauthored my spiritual life from a story governed by the authority of the *bad news* from my family of origin to the authority of the gospel story of the *good news*. They have helped me to face that which I avoided for years, to bear that which was unbearable, and to have trust and faith beyond my fears and anxieties. I hope that some of these concerns, and others that you will raise from your own journey, will bring further light and love into your life.

Epilogue

The following story is Wayne D. Dyer's adaptation of a story told by Henri J. M. Nouwen:

Imagine this scene if you will. Two babies are *in utero,* confined to the wall of their mother's womb, and they are having a conversation. For the sake of clarity we'll call these twins Ego and Spirit.

Spirit says to Ego, "I know you are going to find this difficult to accept, but I truly believe there is life after birth."

Ego responds, "Don't be ridiculous. Look around you. This is all there is. Why must you always be thinking about something beyond this reality? Accept your lot in life. Make yourself comfortable and forget about all of this life-after-birth nonsense."

Spirit quiets down for a while, but her inner voice won't allow her to remain silent any longer. "Ego, now don't get mad, but I have something else to say. I also believe that there is a Mother."

"A Mother!" Ego guffaws. "How can you be so absurd? You've never seen a Mother. Why can't you accept that this is all there is? The idea of a Mother is crazy. You are here alone with me. This is your reality. Now grab hold of that cord. Go into your corner and stop being so silly. Trust me, there is no Mother."

Spirit reluctantly stops her conversation with Ego, but

her restlessness soon gets the better of her. "Ego," she implores, "please listen without rejecting my idea. Somehow I think those constant pressures we both feel, those movements that make us so uncomfortable sometimes, that continual repositioning and all of that closing in that seems to be taking place as we keep growing, is getting us ready for a place of glowing light, and we will experience it very soon."

"Now I know you are absolutely insane," replies Ego. "All you've ever known is darkness. You've never seen light. How can you even contemplate such an idea? Those movements and pressures you feel are your reality. You are a distinct separate being. This is your journey. Darkness and pressures and a closed-in feeling are what life is all about. You'll have to fight it as long as you live. Now grab your cord and please stay still."

Spirit relaxes for a while, but finally she can contain herself no longer. "Ego, I have only one more thing to say and then I'll never bother you again."

"Go ahead," Ego responds impatiently.

"I believe all of these pressures and all of this discomfort is not only going to bring us to a new celestial light, but when we experience it, we are going to meet Mother face-to-face and know an ecstasy that is beyond anything we have ever experienced up until now."

"You really are crazy, Spirit. Now I'm truly convinced of it."[9]

This story contains a central truth of this book. We as persons get stuck, locked in, and fixated on a certain point of view about reality, and we, like Ego, have great difficulty developing an alternative reading of reality. Spiritual transformation involves the capacity to face our confined human perspective, to look beyond our limited experience, and often, to transcend what our primary relationships have negatively taught us about the world and about ourselves. We are invited to be like Spirit and to expect and to seek out a new reality, a new creation, and Another whom we have not yet encountered fully.

Notes

Chapter 1. Introduction

1. Luke 14:26, New Revised Standard Version.
2. Carl Jung, quoted by Ronald Richardson in *Family Ties That Bind* (North Vancouver: Self-Counsel Press, 1984), 1.
3. Ibid., 2.
4. Michael Harter, S.J., ed., *Hearts on Fire: Praying with Jesuits* (St. Louis: Institute of Jesuit Sources, 1993), 9.
5. J. V. Langmead Casserley, *The Christian in Philosophy* (New York: Charles Scribner's Sons, 1951), 42.

Chapter 2. Whose Are You?

1. Thomas Merton, *Bread in the Wilderness* (New York: New Directions, 1953), 76.
2. Merle Jordan, "Prayer and Meditation in Pastoral Care and Counseling," in *Handbook for Basic Types of Pastoral Care and Counseling*, ed. Howard Stone and William Clements (Nashville: Abingdon Press, 1991).
3. Peter Taylor Forsyth, *The Soul of Prayer* (London: Independent Press, 1916), 81–92.
4. Luke 22:42, Revised Standard Version.
5. Charles P. Cohen and Vance R. Sherwood, *Becoming a Constant Object in Psychotherapy with the Borderline Patient* (New York: Jason Aronson, 1991), 13.
6. Julian of Norwich, *Showings* (New York: Paulist Press, 1978).

Chapter 3. Understanding Your Family of Origin

1. Claudia Black, *It Will Never Happen to Me* (New York: Ballantine, 1987).

2. Louis B. Fierman, *The Therapist Is the Therapy* (Northvale, N.J.: Jason Aronson Inc., 1997), 4.

3. Genesis 3:12, Revised Standard Version.

4. Edwin Friedman, "Bowen Theory and Therapy," in *Handbook of Family Therapy,* ed. Alan Gurman and David Kniskern (New York: Brunner/Mazel Publishers), 1991.

5. Albert Ellis, *Humanistic Psychotherapy: The Rational Emotive Approach* (New York: Julian Press, 1973), 55–62.

6. Stephen R. Covey, *The Seven Habits of Highly Effective People* (New York: Simon & Schuster, 1989), 71.

7. Everett L. Shostrom, *Man the Manipulator* (Nashville: Abingdon Press, 1967).

8. From a workshop, "Intergenerational Family Therapy," in La Jolla, California, 1992, with Donald Williamson and James Framo.

9. Louise Armstrong and Whitney Darrow, *A Child's Guide to Freud* (New York: Simon & Schuster, 1963).

10. Robert Llewellyn, *Love Bade Me Welcome* (New York: Paulist Press, 1984), 1.

11. Matthew 5:4, King James Version.

12. Ephesians 4:26, New Revised Standard Version.

13. François Fenelon, in *Christian Perfection,* ed. Charles F. Whiston, 205 (New York: Harper & Brothers, 1947).

14. Psalms 51:4, King James Version.

15. Paul Tournier, *Guilt and Grace* (New York: Harper & Row, 1962).

16. Erich Fromm, *The Art of Loving* (New York: Harper & Brothers, 1956).

17. A. H. Maslow and Bela Mittelman, *Principles of Abnormal Psychology* (New York: Harper & Brothers, 1941), 6.

18. David C. Jacobsen, *Clarity in Prayer* (Corte Madera, Calif: Omega Books, 1976), 93.

19. Judith V. Jordan, Alexandra G. Kaplan, Jean Baker Miller, Irene P. Stiver, and Janet L. Surrey, *Women's Growth in Connection* (New York: Guilford Press, 1991).

20. Tournier, *Guilt and Grace,* 167.

21. Monica McGoldrick and Randy Gerson, *Genograms in Family Assessment* (New York: W. W. Norton & Co., 1985).

22. Menninger Video Productions, *Constructing the Multigenerational Family Genogram: Exploring a Problem in Context* (Topeka: The Menninger Clinic, 1983).

Chapter 4. Facing the Lasting Effects from Your Family of Origin

1. Stephen Prior, *Object Relations in Severe Trauma: Psychotherapy of the Sexually Abused Child* (Northvale, N.J.: Jason Aronson, 1996).

2. Joseph Weiss, *How Psychotherapy Works: Process and Technique* (New York: Guilford Press, 1993).

3. Matthew 5:4, King James Version

4. Joseph Weiss, "Plan Formulation," Steps 1, 5 (Private Clinical Document).

5. Ibid., 3.

6. Weiss, *How Psychotherapy Works*, 13.

7. Ibid., 12.

8. Robert Firestone, *Voice Therapy—A Psychotherapeutic Approach to Self-Destructive Behavior* (New York: Human Sciences Press, 1968), 33.

9. Ibid., 33.

10. Ibid., 35.

11. Robert Firestone, *Suicide and the Inner Voice* (Thousand Oaks, Calif.: Sage Publications, 1997), xii.

12. Firestone, *Voice Therapy*, 18.

13. Robert Firestone, *Combating Destructive Thought Processes: Voice Therapy and Separation Theory* (Thousand Oaks, Calif.: Sage Publications, 1997), 77.

14. Ibid., 110.

15. Firestone, *Suicide and the Inner Voice*, 182.

16. Firestone, *Voice Therapy*, 263.

17. Firestone, *Combating Destructive Thought Processes*, 186.

18. Henri Nouwen, *Life of the Beloved* (New York: Crossroad 1992), 26–27.

19. Firestone, *Voice Therapy*, 205–7.

20. Wilfried Daim, "On Depth-Psychology and Salvation," *Journal of Psychotherapy as a Religious Process*, 2, 1 (January 1955): 28.

21. Ibid., 26.

22. Anna Freud and O. Burlingham, *Kriegskinder* (London: Imago, 1949), 41.

23. Wilfried Daim, *Depth Psychology and Salvation* (New York: Ungar, 1963), 94.

24. Daim, "On Depth-Psychology and Salvation," 29–30.

25. Ibid., 32.

26. Daim, *Depth Psychology and Salvation*, 46–47.

27. Daim, "On Depth-Psychology and Salvation," 34.

28. Daim, *Depth Psychology and Salvation*, 185–87.

29. Daim, "Depth Psychology and Grace," *Journal of Psychotherapy as a Religious Process* 1 (January 1954): 36–37.

30. Daim, *Depth Psychology and Salvation*, 246.

31. Margaret Paul, *Inner Bonding* (San Francisco: HarperCollins, 1992), xi–xii.

32. Ibid.

33. Ibid.

34. Bruce Ecker and Laurel Hulley, *Depth Oriented Brief Therapy*, Video Viewer's Manual (Oakland: Pacific Seminars, 1998), 2.

35. Bruce Ecker and Laurel Hulley, *Depth Oriented Brief Therapy* (San Francisco: Jossey-Bass, 1996), 3.

36. Insoo Kim Berg and Scott D. Miller, *Working with the Problem Drinker: A Solution-Focused Approach* (New York: W. W. Norton & Co., 1992), 13.

37. Ibid., 17.

38. Daniel Taylor, *The Healing Power of Stories* (New York: Doubleday, 1996), 1.

39. Michael White and David Epston, *Narrative Means to Therapeutic Ends* (New York: W. W. Norton & Co., 1990), 40.

40. Ibid., 38.

41. John Byng-Hall, *Rewriting Family Scripts* (New York: Guilford Press, 1995), 9.

42. Alan Parry and Robert E. Doan, *Story Re-visions: Narrative*

Therapy in the Postmodern World (New York: Guilford Press, 1994), 45.

43. Matthew 5:21, 23, King James Version.
44. Peter Taylor Forsyth, *The Principle of Authority* (London: Hodder & Stoughton, 1913), 83.

Chapter 5. Rewriting Your Work, Leadership, and Caregiving Patterns

1. Edwin H. Friedman, *Generation to Generation: Family Process in Church and Synagogue* (New York: Guilford Press, 1985), 3.
2. Ibid., 3.
3. David N. Ulrich and Harry P. Dunne, Jr., *To Love and Work: A Systemic Interlocking of Family, Workplace and Career* (New York: Brunner/Mazel, 1986), xii, xiii.
4. Igor A. Caruso, *Existential Psychology: From Analysis to Synthesis* (New York: Herder & Herder, 1964), 170.
5. Merle Jordan and Wayne Kendall, "Deactivating Pastoral Hot Buttons," unpublished article.
6. Thomas R. Kelly, *A Testament of Devotion* (New York: Harper & Brothers, 1941), 96–97.

Chapter 6. Renewing Your Spirit by Reauthoring Your Childhood Story

1. 1 John 5:21, The Amplified Bible.
2. Peter Taylor Forsyth, *The Principle of Authority* (London: Hodder & Stoughton, 1913), 343.
3. Donald Williamson, *The Intimacy Paradox* (New York: Guilford Press, 1991), 127–50.
4. 1 John 4:16, The Amplified Bible.
5. Henri Nouwen, *Life of the Beloved* (New York: Crossroad, 1992), 25–31.
6. Psalms 51:4, Revised Standard Version.
7. François Fenelon, *Christian Perfection* (New York: Harper & Brothers, 1947).
8. Ibid., 178–79.
9. Wayne Dyer, *Your Sacred Self* (New York: HarperCollins, 1995), 1–2.

Bibliography

Abrams, Jeremiah, ed. *Reclaiming the Inner Child.* Los Angeles: Jeremy Tarcher, 1990.

Daim, Wilfried. *Depth Psychology and Salvation.* Translated and edited by Kurt F. Reinhard. New York: Ungar, 1963.

Denton, Donald Jr. *Religious Diagnosis in a Secular Society.* Lanham, Md.: University Press of America, 1998.

De Shazer, Steve. *Clues: Investigating Solutions in Brief Therapy.* New York: W. W. Norton & Co., 1988.

Ecker, Bruce, and Laurel Hulley. *Depth Oriented Brief Therapy.* San Francisco: Jossey-Bass, 1996.

Firestone, Robert. *Voice Therapy.* New York: Human Sciences Press, 1988.

———. *Combating Destructive Thought Processes.* Thousand Oaks, Calif.: Sage Publications, 1997.

Friedman, Edwin. *Generation to Generation: Family Process in Church and Synagogue.* New York: Guilford Press, 1985.

Gerkin, Charles. *The Living Human Document.* Nashville: Abingdon Press, 1984.

Howe, Leroy. *The Image of God: A Theology for Pastoral Care and Counseling.* Nashville: Abingdon Press, 1995.

Jordan, Merle. *Taking on the Gods.* Nashville: Abingdon Press, 1986.

Lang, Martin. *Acquiring Our Image of God: Emotional Basis for Religious Education.* New York: Paulist Press, 1983.

Leavy, Stanley. *In the Image of God: A Psychoanalyst's View.* New Haven, Conn.: Yale University Press, 1988.

McGoldrick, Monica, and Randy Gerson. *Genograms in Family Assessment.* New York: W. W. Norton & Co., 1985.

Miller, Scott, and Insoo Kim Berg. *The Miracle Method.* New York: W. W. Norton & Co. 1995.

Mogenson, Greg. *God Is a Trauma.* Dallas: Spring Publications, 1989.

Nouwen, Henri. *Life of the Beloved.* New York: Crossroad, 1992.

Oden, Thomas. *The Structure of Awareness.* Nashville: Abingdon Press, 1969.

Paul, Margaret. *Inner Bonding: Becoming a Loving Adult to Your Inner Child.* San Francisco: HarperCollins, 1992.

Prior, Stephen. *Object Relations in Severe Trauma.* Northvale, N.J.: Jason Aronson, 1996.

Richardson, Ronald. *Family Ties That Bind.* North Vancouver: Self-Counsel Press, 1984.

Rizzuto, Ana-Maria. *The Birth of the Living God.* Chicago: University of Chicago Press, 1979.

Ryan, Dale, and Juanita Ryan. *Recovery from Distorted Images of God.* Downers Grove, Ill.: InterVarsity Press, 1990.

Ulrich, David, and Harry Dunne. *To Love and Work: A Systemic Interlocking of Family, Workplace, and Career.* New York: Brunner/Mazel, 1986.

Weiss, Joseph. *How Psychotherapy Works.* New York: Guilford Press, 1993.

White, Michael, and David Epston. *Narrative Means to Therapeutic Ends.* New York: W. W. Norton & Co., 1990.

Whitfield, Charles. *Healing the Child Within.* Deerfield Beach, Fla: Health Communications, 1989.

Williamson, Donald. *The Intimacy Paradox: Personal Authority in the Family System.* New York: Guilford Press, 1991.

Printed in the United States
38313LVS00007B/13-15